GRAINS OF SALT AND RAYS OF LIGHT

GILLIAN CROW

Grains of Salt
and
Rays of Light

Reflections on St Matthew's Gospel

ST PAULS

ST PAULS
Middlegreen, Slough SL3 6BT, United Kingdom
Moyglare Road, Maynooth, Co. Kildare, Ireland

© ST PAULS (UK) 1994
Foreword © Metropolitan Anthony of Sourozh, 1994

ISBN 085439 479 6

Printed by The Guernsey Press Co Ltd, Guernsey, C.I.

ST PAULS is an activity of the priests and brothers of the Society of St Paul who proclaim the Gospel through the media of social communication

Contents

Foreword

St Seraphim of Sarov, a Russian saint of the nineteenth century, said one should read the Holy Scriptures on one's knees; not necessarily physically on one's knees but with a sense of reverence, as though we were on our knees before the Living God who is going to speak to us. St John Chrysostom says that we should not even touch the Book of the Gospel without washing our hands. Again, he does not speak only of a physical ablution; but we must handle this book as something holy.

An icon is as it were the Name of God expressed in line and colour. The Gospel is the Name of God expressed in words; the icon of God in words. The Gospel is God's own word, it is God speaking to us. One the other hand the word of God is not only a semantic word; it is a Person. It is not only the words of God but Christ, in our presence. We are in the presence of Christ, listening while he speaks or venerating him when he is silent, or standing in awe even when the words he speaks are not addressed to us, when others hear the words that are beyond our understanding.

There are moments when we read the word and it speaks to us directly. There are moments when we have an inkling of what it could mean; then we can store it in our heart and mind – but our heart first of all, in the core of our being, not the seat of our emotions – waiting for the moment when we will be mature enough to hear and respond. And there are sad moments when we can only shrug our shoulders or shake our head and say, 'I can't even begin to understand what my Lord and God says. How far I am still from his mind and heart and will and vision.'

These are approaches which are important when we read the Scriptures – this attitude of worship, of adoration when we approach them, physically by reading or by opening the book, and also by listening. But we must also remember an old saying that one does not understand the Scriptures by using only one's mind. It is by becoming the doers of what the Scriptures teach us that we begin to understand the meaning of the words spoken by God in Christ.

So the first step in our reading the Gospel is to try to understand the mind of Christ as expressed in these words. Then in prayer, in surrender, in the doing, in growing into an ever-deepening and widening communion with God, we must try to acquire the mind of Christ so that our actions should gush from within us, not in an act of submissiveness but in an act of communion.

That is the attitude of the faithful, humble disciple who listens with all his or her being. The first thing we must do is to keep alive in us the sense of discipleship. We must remember that there was a moment when we were captured by the personality of the Master, the only One, the Lord Jesus Christ; that we have found that there is no other master one can follow from earth to heaven, from death into eternal life; and that there is no other way than by following the Master who is the truth, who is life, but who is also the way. That implies, of course, that we must by an act of will, by compelling ourselves at moments of slackness or laziness or illness, to come into the presence of God, even if all we can know of this presence is, subjectively speaking, his absence – that as far as we are concerned we perceive nothing of this presence. Yet by faith we know he is here, we know that we stand before him and that he never abandons us.

And then we must read; not read pages, read a very small portion of the Gospel and ask ourselves, 'What have I read? What does this particular passage of the Gospel mean – not on my terms but in God's own term? What did he want to convey to me – not what I want to read into it?'

That is a very big temptation and it requires great integrity and self-discipline to look at a passage and say, 'I make myself completely open. I know not what he wanted to say. I will ask him.'

In order to do this, many spiritual writers tell us to read the passage time and again. Repeat it to yourself, learn it by heart, so that it enters into your mind, so that it reaches you as deeply as possible, and then ask yourself what do these words mean? What does this phrase mean? What was the mind that coined the phrase, what was the heart that poured it out to me, for my salvation? And it may take hours, it may take days to come to a real perception of just one passage.

We have no need of moving away from one passage to find another one until the passage and we have identified. It is easy to read a passage glibly, to take its message for what it appears to be and to go on to another passage and another. And yet we know from the lives of the Desert Fathers and from the lives of the saints that they built all their saintliness on one phrase at times – but one phrase which they took in and of which they made life.

We do not have the wholeness, the integrity, the simplicity of the Desert Fathers, we do not have their desperate need to become alive, to move from death into life. But we must come to enough understanding to realise that this is the only way in which we can bring the message of the Gospel to ourselves: by reading and reading, by repeating and rehearsing in our minds the same words until they are so deeply graven in us, so deeply interwoven with us, that we can begin to live by them.

We must allow ourselves to identify with the word of God, God's message to us, and allow God to become the Lord of our life, the Life of our life.

Metropolitan Anthony
of Sourozh

Introduction

These meditations on the Gospel according to St Matthew grew out of a diary I kept following my own daily Bible reading. They do not therefore form a comprehensive study of each passage, nor a commentary, but are personal reflections; thoughts that came to me on a particular day – fresh, unique perhaps to that occasion, sparks of meaning in a verse which might speak a different message tomorrow.

Yet however personal these meditations are, they inevitably have their roots in the mind and experience of the Church of which I am part. The end result may be mine – individual, imprecise, speculative – but it was cradled in the milieu which has moulded my own faith. Each day I read the Gospel as part of my morning prayers, and in both my prayers and my reading I am conscious of joining with my brothers and sisters in Christ in a corporate act of worship, however physically separated we may be. It is out of their prayer as much as my own that these words come.

To read the Gospel is to hear Christ speak – not only to the fishermen of Galilee, the throngs in the Temple, the lame and the blind – but to us, now, individually. This is our perfect answer to prayer. 'Thy will be done,' we say, and then in the Gospel the Lord spells out his will for us in words that are clear, direct, compelling – and meant for us to fulfil, on this day that we read them.

Yet it is much easier to skim over familiar phrases and hear them addressed to long-dead Pharisees. To weigh every word in the light of ourselves is painful and demanding. It is far less risky to imagine the crowds at Jesus' feet and to admire the beauty of the Beatitudes in a pious way than to realise he is calling me, today, to show mercy and to accept if necessary to be reviled in his name.

We read with our eyes; perhaps our minds are partially engaged; but our hearts and our wills often remain asleep. That is not why the Lord gave us the Gospel. Nor did he intend it to be an academic treatise; scholarly hair-splitting does not provide the inspiration for acting on his words. We must instead delve deep into both the message and our hearts, with all the intensity of which we are capable. We must listen attentively to Christ's voice, hear the nuances behind the words, see the love in his eyes and at the core of our being accept to be moved by what he says to us. These meditations are some of the ways in which his words have moved me, offered as starting-points for your own delving.

They follow the order of St Matthew's Gospel, which is arranged systematically. Within the obvious framework of Christ's ancestry, birth, ministry and death the evangelist groups together subjects such as the Lord's teaching – the Sermon on the Mount; time spent in Jerusalem – the Kingdom parables; and so on. Clarity takes precedence over strict chronological adherence because it is the expounding of the divine message which is of paramount importance, not the day by day recording of Jesus' every move. In an era of no newspaper reports, no television, no mass communication at all bar word of mouth Christ must have repeated the essence of his teaching in village after village, synagogue after synagogue. Sometimes examples of this repetition have come down to us, for instance the command for us to take up our cross, which occurs at two places in the Gospel; and a succession of healing miracles, even two instances of multiplication of loaves and fish. I have taken each passage as it comes in Matthew, and when something is repeated I have looked at it with new eyes the second time.

That must have been the case with the disciples as they listened to the Lord retell a parable or restore another blind man's sight. Words they had heard previously suddenly took on a deeper meaning, their own eyes were progressively opened by seeing the same miracle performed again and again. Repetition is one of the most important ways a child learns; and it is with the humility of children that we should approach our faith, Christ tells us.

We must also regain something of their sense of wonder, laying aside our jaded attitude to both the world around us and the infinite world of the spirit. Very often we have lost the freshness and the impact of the Gospel stories because we have traded our ability to be bowled over by the divine for what we see as an 'adult' scepticism. We are unwilling to let the Kingdom flow into our hearts. We reduce the words of the Gospel to text on a page, instead of their being the voice of the Living God calling us today.

Let us start afresh, listening wide-eyed to the Lord Jesus Christ in adoration and attentiveness; and with the determination to put into practice everything we hear him tell us. If we have truly heard him speak we will never be the same again.

Part 1

GOD BECOME MAN

Chapter 1

The Nativity

1-17. The ancestry of Christ

St Matthew's Gospel opens with a genealogy which puts the Lord Jesus Christ firmly at the head of Mosaic tradition. It is a passage we tend to skip – unless called upon to read it publicly, when all those impossible names send us scurrying off to practise well in advance. Otherwise we are conscious of a long list beginning with Abraham and ending with Christ, and the rest, it seems is largely immaterial. In these days of efficient public records and the classless society the quoting of a pedigree does not have much relevance to us.

It did to Matthew's original readers. Judaism is a matter of family. One is not Jewish because of the place of one's birth or personal religious conviction but by heredity. The Messiah, the Anointed One of Israel, had to satisfy genealogical demands. To us brought up to accept Jesus as the Christ his Messiahship is obvious; to people in the first century that was not the case.

I was struck recently by hearing a Jewish convert to Christianity talking about Jesus' fulfilment of the Old Testament as a matter of overwhelming importance. This is something we cradle Christians often forget or ignore. We see our faith as a new religion, breaking away from the fetters of the Old Testament Law just as there is a break between Old and New Testaments. Christ supersedes rather than fulfils.

This passage can be a valuable reminder that it is not so. Jesus is indeed the fulfilment of the entire Old Testament.

From Abraham, through David to the last of the righteous of Israel – and finally through the two link figures straddling the Old and New Covenants, John the Baptist and Mary – Jesus the Christ stands at the head of the Chosen People, summing up and completing all the Law and the Prophets. The entire Old Testament is focused on him. If we want to find ultimate sense in the Hebrew Scriptures, we have only to read this genealogy.

In my Church this passage is read on the Sunday before the Feast of the Nativity, when we remember with veneration these human ancestors of Christ; people whose destiny was to bring flesh and blood, with their spirits, as an offering to God, playing their part in the divine purpose in an undreamt-of way.

We can take this to heart when the direction of our lives seems unclear. God is fulfilling his divine purpose in and through me today. It may not be given to me to see it but that is not my function. My immediate sights can be fixed unswervingly on doing his will at the present moment – joyfully, lovingly. The overall plan may not be my concern. But just as Christ is at the head of this genealogy, at the head of the entire Old Testament, so he is the Head of the Church, guiding both my life and the direction of the world.

18-25. *Worshipping at the manger*

The Christmas narrative, so familiar, challenges us intellectually and spiritually.

The angel appearing to Joseph tells him to call the child 'Jesus'; but the quotation from Isaiah refers to the name 'Emmanuel'. We know that this is totally descriptive of the Lord – it means 'God with us', assuring us of his presence and support. It also assures us, here on the very first page of the New Testament, that Jesus is truly God.

That is reminiscent of the beginning of St John's Gospel where we learn that Jesus Christ, the Word, was 'with

God' – in the divine Trinitarian union with the Father and the Spirit – from all eternity. Here we discover that without ceasing to be at one with God, he lays aside the glory which was his before the world was, to become 'with us'. He unites divinity with humanity in a decisive and irreversible way.

So 'Emmanuel' sums up the Incarnation: the almighty, distant and totally Other God of Israel with a name too holy to be pronounced has humbled himself to become one of us – frail, vulnerable, sharing the precarious human condition.

This self-emptying should strike us as something awesome. The Baby Jesus in the manger, around which one can stand and coo fondly, is too comfortable a picture. Certainly the ordinariness of the Nativity is very precious and beautiful. Christ sharing our human life, becoming a babe in arms is something to which we can all relate. But the tendency is to relate on a purely sentimental level – witness all those tacky Christmas cards – and to lose our awareness of Jesus' divinity. That paves the way for the popular denial of him as being anything other than a wise but ordinary human being.

Where would that leave us? Jesus seen just as a prophet or teacher, nothing but a man, cannot preach the God of Love whom we know; because the remote God who keeps his distance from his creation could not be the God of the Christian message.

Christ is fully man, fully God – the old paradox which frightens many modern theologians. It offends their arrogant intellectualism because it is too great a concept to be mastered by the human mind. All we can do is to worship in awe, in wonder, in gratitude.

This is what the simple shepherds did at Bethlehem. It is also, Matthew tells us, what the Magi did – those men who were at the forefront of the scientific-religious thought of their day. They did not coo. They worshipped. They approached this tiny helpless infant as a king, falling down before him. They were prepared to put their dignity on the line with a certainty that puts most of us to shame.

19

There is another side to the awesomeness of the Nativity. The white swaddling bundle lying in the darkness of the cave of Bethlehem prefigures the dead Christ shrouded in the tomb of Calvary. The Nativity spells salvation for us – at a price God has already undertaken to pay.

If we dare to come to the manger of Bethlehem, must it not be with the realisation that here, today, before my world-weary eyes God has entered history in a decisive, glorious but tragic way? Against the shining background of singing angels and reverent kings we find the squalor of the cowshed, a life begun and to continue in poverty, rejection and the acceptance of vulnerability even to death.

It is a picture of humility on all sides; the perfect humility of Christ, the lesser humility of those who would put aside status to worship in a stable, to lay at an infant's feet their material, intellectual and spiritual possessions as a gift to him. Can we do the same?

From Matthew's account of the Nativity we can catch a glimpse of Joseph. He is, we learn 'just'. But do not his thoughts go further than justice? He does not wish this young pregnant girl to whom he is betrothed to be put to shame. His justice is seasoned with mercy and kindness. It is real justice – not a legalistic selfishness aimed at being in the right at all costs, never mind who gets hurt; but a heartfelt desire that good may prevail.

The second thing we learn is that he responded absolutely to the angel in his dream – one gets the impression immediately. His faith is one of total trust, total obedience, total intention to act on God's orders. It is true faith – faithfulness to God's will.

All this is done against a background of possible scandal and finger-pointing which he withstands solidly, relying on God rather than men. This is real integrity, lived out in circumstances which would provoke most of us to make excuses. It is only possible when one's sights are fixed not on worldly glory but on God himself.

So there is much that Joseph can teach us. If we find the demands of the Gospel out of present reach we can at least start here, with someone who had such an enormous challenge before he had seen the Resurrection, before the New Covenant, while still living under the Law. Here is a man who can already transcend the strictures of the Law and so enable Christ the fulfilment of the Law to come to us.

Chapter 2

Jesus' early life

1-12. Herod

King Herod, like so many rulers titled 'the Great' was a megalomaniac who immortalised himself with technically amazing building works – witness today the breathtaking remains of Masada – and a reputation for cruelty.

Yet this great man was intimidated by the Magi's words.

After enquiries he makes a treacherous pact with them; if they will sus out this new-born threat to his power he will come and...? He tells them 'worship' but they are warned about his real motives.

Why did he not simply follow the star himself? He was no star-watcher, he might have replied. The truth was he had no intention of meeting the Christ child face to face. His minions with their swords would do that. He just wanted the necessary information.

Perhaps the most shocking thing about Herod is his faith. He does not need to see the Messiah before his eyes. He is quite prepared to accept the Magi's word. Later in the Gospel we will find the same kind of perverted faith; the scribes and the Pharisees sought to kill Jesus not because they doubted his miracles but precisely because they believed in them.

Like Herod they saw Christ as a powerful enemy to be feared and hated, for all their cries of unbelief in him. This demonic fear of God, this demonic kind of faith, is something of which we should be more aware. It is the opposite of the good faith spoken of by Christ, which is a love-response to Love. And it is Love, divine and Incarnate, by which we are saved.

13-23. Egypt and Nazareth

The flight into Egypt is something of a bridge, linking the Christmas story to Jesus' adulthood. It tells us absolutely nothing about his upbringing, his family life, his childhood experience of exile in Egypt or his early career as a provincial craftsman, facing all the trials and frustrations of any other small town inhabitant during the Roman occupation of Palestine.

This not knowing has its effect on us. We are told that the Gospels set out what is necessary for us to learn for our salvation. What Christ had for dinner, what his favourite colour was, even what he looked like are not things we need to know at all.

Yet in another very real sense we do. First, because there is a pernicious view held by some Christians that if it's not in the Bible it can't be true. This is plainly nonsense; but a few more written details would be more acceptable to some people than suppositions which may be true but which have no scriptural authority.

Second, because there is a natural tendency for us to reduce our view of Jesus to the figure we see in his ministry – miracle-worker, teacher, leader. We lose sight of the child, the teenager, the peasant artisan. It may be easy to practice what you preach when you are a famous rabbi but what about being perfect when you're a kid among the local village ruffians, or a carpenter being hassled by impatient customers and wood that won't plane true? What was Jesus the nobody like? We modern nobodies would like to know.

The only glimpses we get, apart from Luke's account of the childhood incident in the Temple, are odd remarks Christ makes during his ministry. When he speaks of good measure 'pressed down, shaken together, running over' (Lk 6:38) we can perhaps envisage him running childhood errands to the market place, watching the flour heaped up by a trader recommended by his mother – 'go to so-and-so, he always gives good measure'. We can see him watching the dough rise or going to the aid of Joseph to remove a splinter from his eye. We can see him sitting in the square playing games with the other children, aware of the sulkers who refuse to join in however you try to humour them. We know that he learnt to read and that he attended the synagogue week by week. We have to assume that he ate up his meals, washed behind his ears and went to the loo the same as the rest of us.

Because if we pretend he didn't, we dissolve away his humanity to be left with a divine figure who had only the semblance of a man. We are modern-day docetists, heretics of a most dangerous kind.

The same attitude lies behind the outlook often expressed by people who speak in adamant terms about not knowing what Christ looked like. The Bible does not tell us, it is true. But there are icons from the early centuries showing a dark-haired, dark-eyed Jewish face which, if not photographically accurate, cannot be far wrong. What is certainly wrong is the insistence that it is not given to us humans to know what he looked like, as if the Incarnation had never .ken place. No! Thousands of real and ordinary people saw his face, knew exactly the shape of his nose, the look in his eye, the way he smiled. His appearance was not unknowable, like the remote God of the Old Testament. He was visible flesh and blood, with the experience of everyday life common to us all.

Matthew does not spell out the details – not because they were not there, but because we ought to be sufficiently mature in our faith to assume the truth beyond the written text.

So this brief episode, encompassing thirty years in a handful of sentences, should not be seen as a negative thing. Our own lives are largely made up of years and years which abound in boring minutiae over which history will pass without even a mention. And yet it was these very years which formed us, which were our gift from God, which we used as best we could without being in any way spectacular.

When we are tempted to wonder what we are doing here, what possible purpose we can have in the divine plan, these hidden years of the Saviour can be a real source of inspiration. God himself was content to live a humdrum, ordinary life like mine. He experienced all my frustrations, my responsibilities and pressures, with no compensation of stardom. He bore them all with love, with equanimity and with thirty long years of patience. That is all just as much a part of the Gospel of our salvation as is the Cross and the resurrection.

Chapter 3

The new life of Baptism

1-12. John the Baptist

If the Gospels give us no indication of Jesus' appearance they do at least describe his cousin John. They stress the unusual aspects – the rough clothing, the strange diet, both belonging to the ascetic life of a desert hermit.

He was a compelling and unforgettable figure. His message touched the hearts of multitudes, but so too did his appearance and his lifestyle. Isaiah called him prophetically a 'voice' but the Gospels give that voice flesh and blood. What we see of John is the whole man – he is not a disembodied voice but a powerful character who lives his message in body and soul.

His words are clear, hard-hitting, fearless. He does not peddle a comfortable religion. He is as ruggedly uncompromising as the scorching Judaean landscape.

He challenged the people of his day to repentance, that is to a complete change of direction, away from sin and towards God, to a life which would bear fruit. How does he challenge us?

I think we can learn from what John was. 'A voice', the Gospel calls him. He put his whole self into his message, counting himself and his personal life as little in the light of his vocation.

So far so good. I can understand that we should identify with the Good News to such an extent that we should become its embodiment. But should our self-effacing identification mean complete loss of our identity, so that in becoming living mouthpieces of God we cease to be ourselves? Does being a voice mean being nothing but a disembodied voice, depersonalized like interchangeable zombies?

I don't think so. What is so remarkable about John is precisely his individuality, his memorable appearance and personality as a vibrant human being. It is true that his physical description has a definite purpose, echoing that of Elijah whom he represents. Nevertheless, this passage shows us that John, even seen as a second Elijah, was also – intensely – John. He had given his life, his whole being to God; and God had not dissolved him away into a character-less tool whose individuality had been swallowed up. It had been hallowed and given back to him a hundredfold.

That is very important for us to remember. So often I am aware of a latent fear, in myself and others, that giving ourselves totally to God will result in the loss of everything we hold most dear: not just possessions, not just our lives, but us, our individuality, our personhood. Is that not what we see around us all the time on a human level? We give ourselves unreservedly to a person we love – parent, child, partner – and our self-sacrifice results in being swallowed up and destroyed.

All too often human love has this devouring quality. If that is our only experience we may imagine that divine love will be similar; and talk of becoming 'a voice' seems to reinforce that idea. God – already fearful in his omnipotence – will likewise swallow us up if we in our loving naiveté surrender to him. His hold on us seems strong enough already. What we would really like to do is to limit it; if on the contrary we give in to it we will be totally consumed.

John's example shows us it is not so. Surrender to God, give your all, he says, and you will find the Kingdom where every person becomes truly fulfiled, truly enabled to become what you are called to be – not a depersonalized clone but the beautiful shining and unique likeness of the Living God.

Like John we will become more of a person, not less. But like him we will have to take that first, daring step into

27

the wilderness of the unknown where we can only survive if we have perfect trust in God.

13-17. Jesus' baptism

The Baptism of Christ in the Jordan is one of the great events in the story of our salvation. It is the culmination of the revelation begun at the Annunciation. Then the mystery of the Incarnation is made known only to his Mother. At the Nativity he becomes visible to humanity represented by the shepherds and the Magi. At his baptism the revelation is completed as he initiates his ministry to all.

John the Baptist announces Christ's coming, preparing the people by calling them to repentance, a process still valid for us today. Repentance is our first act on becoming Christians. Then on a day-to-day basis we learn to confess our sins, privately or publicly, as a prelude to prayer or receiving Communion. Perhaps we become blasé about it as we grow older. We no longer see the urgency which John proclaimed.

'Then Jesus came from Galilee to the Jordan to John, to be baptized by him.' This should pull us up short. All my routine prayers of repentance, salted with half-hearted apology and inadequate attention, come from a sinner. Here we have Christ himself, perfect, coming forward to make what appears to be a public act of repentance. And he doesn't just pop into the nearest convenient synagogue. He has to walk – miles – in order to answer this call which, logically, should not even apply to him.

Why? Is it just so that he can make a public statement about beginning his ministry, and that the Trinity can be revealed in the voice of the Father, the Spirit's descent in the form of a dove, and the Son's immersion in the Jordan? I have heard some beautiful thoughts on this passage. One of them likens Christ's baptism to a fleece being dipped in dye. When other people enter the water, they are washed of their sins and the water becomes heavy with them as when dye leaks out of clothing that is washed. But then Christ enters the water, he is the pure white fleece which takes up the dye from the others. He comes up out of the water bearing the sins of humanity which have been washed away from us.

That is a very beautiful illustration. Another, complementary image: Christ has taken his body from Mary, he has used her flesh given voluntarily by her to become an innocent child who is both Man and God. In his divinity he has already outside time accepted the full consequences of the Incarnation. But it would be monstrous if his human will and body were not given the freedom to accept or reject these consequences. Here at the Jordan Christ in his perfect manhood takes on his vocation to become one with us in our mortality.

In his perfect love for us he acts decisively in a way which is totally unnecessary for him. He has no need of baptism; sin is radically absent from him. As John realises to his dismay, Christ should be the one who baptizes him; logic and right are turned on their head. In the same way, Christ who is Eternal Life, who cannot therefore fall under the natural law of death, will later submit himself to be crucified, setting aside his omnipotence and the consequences of perfection to take on every human limitation to the ultimate. And this is all not out of necessity, but chosen out of perfect Love.

In 'fulfilling all righteousness' Christ is not acceding to some juridical whim, or the letter of religious observance; nor is he acting to appease a vengeful, bloodthirsty deity. He is fulfilling the law of Love, which is perfect righteousness. He is restoring the relationship of face to face love between God and man which was lost at the Fall and which the Mosaic Law was unable of itself to restore. He is reaching down to his helpless creatures to become God with us, Emmanuel.

Chapter 4

The beginning of Christ's ministry

1-17. The temptation in the wilderness

Christ's temptation in the wilderness is crucial to our salvation. The devil uses the most pious arguments to lead him astray. He quotes Scripture. He speaks a twisted sort of faith: 'If Thou be the Son of God' – which is certainly true. He promises good things; all creation, seen in its glory, the glory given it by God himself.

But truth in itself is not enough. The devil has a knowledge and an understanding of God which puts us to shame. He does not suffer from the half-belief which so often plagues us. He is perfectly willing to admit the Sonship of Christ. He has faith; he has hope – great hope for his own plans.

What he lacks radically is love. He sees the glory of God, and instead of falling down in adoration he suggests the Creator worship him.

In his temptation of Christ he tries to divide the Trinity. Satan is a monad, a creature wholly alone. The Trinity on the other hand is a unity of the three divine Persons united in perfect love. And love knows no separation.

Satan is the antithesis of love. Evil has sometimes been described as a no-thing. Perhaps we could also call it – he – a no-love. Satan is the isolated one, incapable of giving of himself in love, eternally alone despite his demons. He is cut off from fellowship and exists only in impenetrable hatred.

Seeing Satan in those terms perhaps helps to unmask his presence in us. How often he tempts us and we are not even aware of it! We do not recognise the real source of our hatreds and hostilities. We pray not to be led into this confrontation with the evil one because we are not strong enough to withstand it. We cannot answer him with the word that Christ used. Our human frailty is too great. And in that frailty we ask instead for deliverance.

But Christ, too, was a man, as well as God. He faced Satan in his humanity as well as in his divinity. He shows us what we could achieve, if we only follow his example in the power of the Holy Spirit.

But all too often we are too busy bowing down to Satan to look up and see Christ leading us on the narrow way.

18-22. *Hearing the call*

The beginning of Jesus' ministry has a dynamic immediacy. He calls the Galilean fishermen and they respond at once.

'Immediately they left the boat'; 'And he went about all Galilee'; as if it all happened in a flash.

Perhaps it did. We are faced with the arresting presence of the Messiah, the sudden moment of truth; flashes of holy lightening indeed. The disciples can only drop their nets in wonder. But what is missed out is the grey between the flashes. In between each synagogue where Christ preached were miles of road which had to be foot-slogged. What did he and the disciples think, say and do on the way? How did they use the time productively?

How can I use my time productively between 'flashes' of inspiration, between work, social engagements, family commitments? Of what does my personal foot-slogging grey consist? Largely, I fear, indiscipline and sloth, into which I am beguiled because they are comfortable.

We know from elsewhere in the Gospels that Christ in fact used this time on the road to instruct his disciples. It was not wasted in idle chit-chat. A long, slow process of learning and of inner transformation was going on. This is something which is possible for me, too.

31

But first I must immediately leave my nets, my familiar boat, and follow Christ – as decisively as the disciples did.

A thought: do those nets ensnare us as much as the 'fish' we catch? We are held captive to our daily lives, our accustomed inertia. We think we are the ones in control but so often it is we ourselves who are the unwitting victims. Instead of being beguiled by the nets of worldly considerations I should be eternally enmeshed in the nets of the Galilean.

Love must have overwhelmed those first fishermen as they came face to face with Love Incarnate. Immediately their nets dropped out of their hands, they clambered out of the boat, following without question or thought for the future. At first their desire was all. Later, after the grey days on the road, when they began to learn the less dramatic business of day-to-day Christian living in imitation of their Master, they also began to overflow with love.

I have seen that in modern saints, so it is not something given only to the Apostles and impossible for us in the twentieth century. We can have the overflowing of divine love as our attainable goal. But the beginning is to desire it with all one's heart. Lord, enflame us with that desire!

23-25. *Galilee aflame*

Three verses which skim over all Christ's saving work! He taught, he preached, he healed. And great crowds began to follow him. How exciting it must have been! It is so easy for us – indeed, we barely have an alternative – to condense Jesus' ministry into a handful of miracles and a couple of sermons. In reality it went on week in, week out. People whose names, whose very existence have not come down to us were singled out and healed by the Lord, not so that they could be an inspiration to us but simply because he responded to their need. These scant verses speak about an outpouring of love such as has never been seen before or since on the earth. Suddenly this tiny Roman province became alive, in the deepest sense of the word. It was aglow with God.

It is so easy to pass over these verses as merely a link between one big Gospel episode and another. But between the calling of the Apostles and the Sermon on the Mount the world had changed.

That is a reminder to us that we must not make the Gospel – the Good News – too small by confining it to the text on the page, because behind the bare words are a thousand unspoken marvels.

Part 2

TEACHING

Chapter 5

The law of love

1-12. The Beatitudes

I do not like reading the Beatitudes in anything other than the Authorised Version. That is because of my familiarity since childhood with the poetic language, the satisfying cadences, the enticing memorability of these beautiful words – words reinforced each Sunday as I hear them sung at our services, as is the custom in my Church.

The RSV comes acceptably close. But what I really cannot abide is the use in some modern translations of 'happy' instead of 'blessed'.

I know that the original Greek – 'makarioi' – can be translated 'happy', but the English word is so debased and impoverished compared with the Greek. The ancient pagans referred to the dead as 'makarioi'; happy because they had been blessed by the gods in their shadowy version of paradise. They were enjoying a state of bliss which had definite religious connotations.

So if one uses the word 'happy' here it must be seen in the sacred context of being in a state of divine grace – of having received, indeed, God's blessing. It is to have come as little children to the Lord Jesus and to have felt his hands on our heads and his arms around us.

That childlike quality is important. To be poor in spirit, to be meek, to be pure in heart all entail a renunciation of adult sophistication; a return to virtues which all too often we cannot wait to outgrow in our rush to reach the false maturity of the world. Christ warns us again and again of the inevitability of becoming like little children if we wish to enter the Kingdom. Our cynical, worldly-wise attitudes produce a hardness of heart which arm us against the things of God.

When I think of the really impressive Christians I have met, men and women whose kinship with the Lord shines in their personal holiness and in the whole of their lives, I am struck in every case by their simplicity, sense of innocence and wide-eyed wonder and enthusiasm – all qualities found supremely in children.

I am reminded of the way in which young babies behave when they are excited. If you present a hungry baby with his bottle he shows his utter delight by convulsing his whole body in a paroxysm of joy as he throws out his arms and legs in total jerky abandon. Alas! We adults have become so constrained. How rarely do we manage more than a polite word or two when we are pleased? How rarely do we put our whole heart into things, let alone our whole body?

I once gave an old monk some strawberries. When he saw them his entire face began to shine; his eyes popped out in wonder, he pursed his lips in eager anticipation, his voice almost squealed with delight. Anyone would have thought I had given him the moon instead of what was, I have to admit, a rather mediocre box of fruit. But his entire being was in the 'thank you!' he uttered. His was a heart open and ready to receive from God and from humanity, with the simplest joy.

But what such a heart does receive from humanity, all too often, is the other side of the Beatitudes: reviling, persecution, evil. Children are horribly vulnerable, totally unable to defend themselves from the wiles of everyday life. Few of us are prepared to expose ourselves to such a state. We have lost our simple trust in God and learnt to rely on our own strength partly because we feel this is necessary in our godless society. Furthermore, we know that in that society's terms our strategy works. We see the meek and the humble trodden down constantly. We are all too aware that what God promises to bless us with is the torture and degradation of the Cross.

And that does not make us rejoice and be glad. Do I not rather seek approbation, do I not shrink in fear of persecution? Are not my sights fixed on this world only, not on the Kingdom at all? I would really prefer my rewards to be here and now, not in heaven.

But Christ tells us that the Kingdom is here and now. 'Blessed are the poor in spirit, for theirs is the Kingdom of heaven'; present tense. All my self-sufficiency does not produce the sheer joie de vivre of the monk who accepted my strawberries. He went through life genuinely alive to every minute, every opportunity, whether good or ill. Every part of his being was totally responsive. And what he perceived, what made him so alive, was the awareness of the Kingdom – living in him at every moment.

For us who are still hard of heart, the hardness has become as unfeeling and dead as horn. True, that allows us to be pierced by life and remain unhurt, just as we can cut our toenails without feeling any pain. But do we want to become nothing more than toenails on the Body of Christ, and not its living tissue?

Well, to take this strange metaphor a stage further, even toenails can be boiled down to produce that most pliable of substances, gelatine. There is Christian hope for even the hardest of hearts! But are we going to turn ourselves to the warmth of Christ and let ourselves be melted by his gentle words, or will we have to endure a ferocious boiling down because we do not respond spontaneously to the kindly fire of his blessing?

Would we not all like to feel blessed by God? Not happy, in its secular sense, but truly blessed, hallowed creatures who can in childlike beauty receive the Kingdom now?

13-16. Salt and light

Salt and light are two things the Christian is called to be, according to these verses. This has a special significance for me, since because of a permanent medical condition I have a craving for both.

So these words have a very personal ring. Experience has shown how dependent I am on salt and light. Far from being everyday, universal commodities they are, I am aware, essential for our very existence. I know only too clearly, as others may only know theoretically, that their absence spells death.

It is that stark realisation which accompanies my reading of these verses. Unsalted food is not merely less delicious than it could be, or a grey day a disappointing occasion for an outing. We are talking about a saltless planet shrouded in eternal darkness; about the total incapability of sustaining life.

Unless the world contains spiritual salt and light it will also die. And these grains of salt and rays of light which are so fundamental to existence are – we Christians! We are not to be like light, like salt: we are light and salt, the very essence of life. This is not some well-chosen metaphor of Christ's. He is speaking the literal truth.

We have been ordained salt and light. We have taken on the properties of these fundamental substances at our baptism. They are God-given, not something we must strive for if we feel like making the effort, as if they were an optional extra. I am formed, in my faith, of salt and light. If is God's work, not something of which I may boast. What is my function is to give of myself unreservedly, to fill with my life-giving properties everything with which I come in contact. I must be willing to be dissolved into those near me, in total self-offering; I must shine as a beacon on those still at a distance, illuminating their path to Christ. I must bring him so substantially into every situation that the possibility of his loss is seen as the death that it actually is. Godlessness must be revealed as the mortal disease, and the salt and light of the Gospel – made present in us – as its only remedy.

And if Christianity is ignored, trampled underfoot, covered over by the darkness of material concerns so that we become indistinguishable from the world, have we then not lost our very substance? If I refuse to be the salt and light of Christ, do I not doom myself to eternal darkness along with the planet? If we cannot become so filled with the properties of the Saviour that we can say with St Paul that 'it is not I, but Christ who lives within me', then we have no life at all.

17-20. Fulfilling the Law

Christ speaks of his coming to fulfil the Law as something beautiful, holy and joyful, a gift of God to be cherished.

He did not of course keep the petty regulations which had been added to it by men. But he showed the Law for what it truly was: the Law of divine Love.

Inevitably for us much of it refers to what we call civil law – rules for organising and governing society. We have lost the vision of just what sort of law Moses brought down from Sinai: not only a religious edict, a recipe for the spiritual life, but the complete set of laws for a nation to live by. There was no divide between the civil and the religious, since God was Israel's supreme ruler and every detail of daily life, state law and religious observance was to be governed by him.

We Gentiles have our own national laws. So when we talk about the Law of the Old Testament we do, as routine, think in terms of the only part to which we feel an affinity – the obviously 'religious' part. Here we follow the early Church.

But this moral and religious Law has been illumined by Christ and set out in the Gospels in terms accessible to us Gentiles; not redefined but rephrased according to our new power of living in the Holy Spirit.

For here in the Sermon on the Mount Christ repeats the definition of Moses: 'Thou shalt love the Lord thy God... and thy neighbour as thyself' on which commandments all the Law depends.

All we have to do is follow that, as fleshed out in these chapters! If we really love God and our neighbour as ourselves we need not be anxious about the particulars of tithing dill and cumin which pertained to an ancient rural society – we will be so overflowing with generosity that we will have given our all to God.

Oh yes? Does this really happen? Are we not, in fact, worse than the Pharisees, who did at least give their ten per cent? But if we cannot become poor for the sake of our needy neighbour, have we not forfeited the right to call ourselves Christians?

21-30. Conscience

After the poetic beauty of the Beatitudes we come to the hard-hitting stuff. The picture of the person blessed in godliness, the image for us all to live up to, is set aside and Christ comes back to us as we really are: quick to anger instead of merciful; unforgiving instead of radiating peace; lascivious and bitter instead of pure in heart.

It is very easy to find excuses for explaining these words away. Losing my temper is not as bad as bludgeoning someone to death; Christ is speaking figuratively, there is a difference between having wicked thoughts and translating them into action. The very fact that we do not do so shows our Christian restraint.

That reasoning works, on an external level. From an interior viewpoint things look different. Why does the murderer murder or the adulterer steal another man's wife? Because he let himself be ruled by the evil desires in his heart.

If we let our anger rule us we will find ourselves on a slippery slope that ends in violence. If we do not learn to nip evil in the bud then we are laying ourselves open to the devil's embrace. We lose control of ourselves and become the playthings of evil.

In all this we have a friend. Jesus calls him 'the accuser', the one who will prod us at every turn when our thoughts begin to stray: our conscience. If we accept his counsel even when it seems stern, if we can learn to see him as a friend whose advice is to be trusted rather than as a spoilsport, then he will have no word with which ultimately to convict us.

This personification of our conscience – which is how the ancient Fathers read verse 25 – is reminiscent of the Holy Spirit, who comes to convince us of sin. If we open our conscience to the Holy Spirit, listen to his words speaking through it, we will be transformed from twisted creatures outwardly whitewashed but inwardly full of putrefaction and we will begin to shine, from the inside out, with the blessedness of purity of heart.

But there has to be a cutting edge. I know too well how easy it is to blunt one's conscience. Our hearts tell us that a certain course of action is 'wrong'; but our reason applies itself industriously to find ways of justifying it. We invent a whole vocabulary with which to disguise theft as fiddling, lies as economy with the truth, deceit as a cosy little scheme.

When God reverses the process we do not like it. How dare he consider a surreptitious glance at a Page Three picture to be in the same league as adultery? How dare he look into my heart and see the hatred which I disguise as indignation or indifference?

Lord, grant me to see my conscience not as a tiresome adversary but as my friend. Grant me to listen to his words of accusation, to delight in their sharpness and to respond to them with an open and pure heart, and with all my will. Lord, there is only one real Adversary; grant that I may recognise Satan for what he is, the murderer of my conscience.

31-42. Beyond the rules

The Pharisees' attitude to questions of marital fidelity, oaths and retribution all stemmed from their understanding of the Law as a juridical exercise rather than a bond of love.

Throughout this chapter Christ has been calling us to a glorious vision of perfection: of human life as it could be, so shot through with divine blessedness that it attains to heights of God-like love never before considered attainable on earth.

But this exhortation to be perfect is just that: an exhortation, an invitation couched in the seductive language of a love-relationship, not stark commands to be kept out of cold-blooded legalism.

You already have the rules of the Mosaic Law, Christ tells us, but now I am leading you beyond them to the beauty of living in the divine mystery of the Trinity where all is love and mutual self-giving.

While God remained remote in veiled Old Testament splendour humanity was not able to go beyond the rules. Now, in Christ's presence and in the post-Pentecost life of the Church in the Holy Spirit, the veil has been rent, we have gone beyond blind rules to look wide-eyed into the divine Face and see our potential selves reflected there.

Become what you are called to be, my very flesh and blood, Christ invites us. Filled with the divine Spirit you can share my perfected life.

This has nothing to do with our own efforts at rule-keeping; it is a question of accepting, freely, God's grace freely given, in other words of entering into a relationship of love with him.

But this grace, this love-relationship, is cross-shaped, because divine love is sacrificial. To us sinners this can take the shine off the glorious vision offered to us. And as love is always free, never a matter of coercion, so we are free to remain on the level we are able to bear. If that is the one governed by rules, if we cannot proceed beyond 'thou shalt not kill, thou shalt not commit adultery', then God in his tender-hearted mercy will for the moment accept us on that level. He will be content to whisper patiently in our ear, 'beyond, beyond, to me!' every time we read these words.

43-48. *Perfection in love*

To love one's enemies – who can honestly do that? Yet one sees it in the saints, especially the martyrs.

Christ does not say we would not have enemies. He had plenty himself. We should offer the hand of friendship to all – but expect in return that some will turn their backs or oppose us in open hatred. We cannot expect less than our Master, and that is how they treated him.

So we should love those who set themselves up against the good in us. We should pray for our persecutors. Like God we are called to be indiscriminate in our Christian love. Our circumstances can hardly be more extreme than being hammered to a cross and finding the breath and the desire to plead for our tormentors' forgiveness.

This chapter started out so enticingly with the beautiful words of the Beatitudes. We were given a vision of the blessedness of a right relationship with God and our neighbour, a blessedness which was, however to be showered upon us through our trials of persecution and mourning. We have been taken by Christ deeper into this divine mystery of uniting love of God and love of neighbour by our treatment of one another which is to reflect God's own treatment of people – loving, forgiving, generous.

In a word, we are called to reach out to the divine perfection, which was intimated by Moses but which in the person of Christ surpasses any set of rules. He is perfection Incarnate, the living example to follow.

We have been given an attainable goal because we have also been given, along with these words, the Holy Spirit. For us all things are possible if we will only allow ourselves to be willing to be stretched, to be pulled towards that goal of perfection by the Spirit who is able to expand us to infinity.

Chapter 6

Relating to God

1-8. Witness and hypocrisy

The command to give alms and pray in secret presents difficulties. Of course one understands what the Lord means. Hypocrisy bears no relation to Christianity.

Nevertheless there is a problem. If we do all these things in total secrecy we are accused of not practising what we preach – another form of hypocrisy.

An example: I have a wealthy Christian friend who gives the impression that he does not care about the world's starving. For a time I judged him accordingly, before I discovered that in fact he gives substantially to famine relief, but in secret.

Certainly I was wrong to judge. Yet I fear his non-Christian acquaintances make the same mistake, and judge Christianity by the hypocritical standards they think they perceive in him.

The problem is one of witness. We want to witness not to ourselves but to our faith as effectively as we can, and one way of doing that is to show the world that we are not an introverted bunch of dreamers but that we really put our faith into action, that we truly live Christianity; that our faith works.

Perhaps the difficulty lies in the fact that these are all surface issues. A true inner change in our whole being – not just in isolated behaviour – would overflow on everyone around us. If we shone with divine love and compassion it would not be necessary for people to see that we gave to charity or went to church. It is not what my right hand gives that is important; what matters is that I give myself.

9-13. The Lord's Prayer

Sometimes one gets the impression that familiarity has all but killed the Lord's Prayer. We rattle it off parrot-fashion from the infants' school. We analyze it in study groups, we tinker with the translation, changing 'Thou' to 'you' and back again.

Underneath all this activity lurks the guilty feeling that all is not well.

How many books have I read on prayer? Quite a few; to one of them I owe my conversion. But still I feel the need for more, and there are shelves of them waiting in the book shops.

The reason for this compulsive reading is that praying, we are told – and know from experience – is difficult. We humans need all the help we can get to communicate with God. So we turn for advice to other humans who are like us fallen and fallible beings grappling with the Divine.

But the disciples asked God himself how to pray. 'Teach us to pray', they said to the Lord Jesus Christ, as St Luke records. Not 'Give us a prayer'. They did not want mere words; they sought method: 'Teach us how'. And Christ replies, 'Pray then like this'. Whatever we have done with the Lord's Prayer, whatever we continue to make of it, we very rarely see it as a method. It is not just a set piece but the basis for the whole of our prayer life; indeed, for the whole of our life.

I am struck by the parallel between the Lord's Prayer and the Ten Commandments. To say 'Our Father' puts us immediately into a relationship of love between ourselves, God and our neighbour. An 'Almighty God' is powerful but distant, even cold. But Our Father in heaven brings us into the familial Paradise, into the arms of limitless Love

47

divine, the perfect Dad who cherishes us as his infinitely precious children.

Lovely picture though that is, it is not enough. How can we sinful humans, alone of all created beings, dare to call our Creator, on whom we turn our callous backs time and again, 'Father'? We are not sons and daughters of God, either by nature or by behaviour.

Only the Lord Jesus Christ, as the only-begotten Son, can legitimately call God 'Father'. And we can only do the same, enter the same relationship of sonship, to the extent to which we have put on Christ and taken on his life, to become sons and daughters of God by adoption. To say 'Our Father' brings us into the sonship of Christ. We can never say 'my Father'. We must be totally inseparable from Jesus, he must live in us, he must utter 'Our Father' through us.

To say 'Our Father' brings us also into the company of our brothers and sisters, who are at one with us in this beautiful word 'our'. If we exclude our neighbour there is no sonship for us; there is no relationship we can have with God in isolation either from Christ or from each other. We can only come to him if we can so love our neighbour that he or she becomes totally inseparable from us, as if we had given ourselves to be a Siamese twin to him or her.

So only if we love God with all our heart and our neighbour as ourselves according to the commandment and within the life of Christ, only if we are within this sacred family relationship with God and all humanity, can we pray at all in any real sense – that is, enter the Kingdom, where we put aside all false gods and joyfully accept to do the Lord's will.

And that consists in living the Kingdom on earth; in actively putting into practice the remaining commandments, and in giving and receiving forgiveness when in human frailty we and our neighbour fail. If we and our neighbour are one there can be no other way to express our love for him or her.

I become increasingly worried by certain devout Christians who seem to equate prayer only with asking for things, and 'answered prayer' as the be-all and end-all, even as proof that Christianity 'works'. That is a dangerous seeking after what one can get out of God, not a seeking after the Living God himself. It encourages further testing, and ever bigger requests, not a deeper love-relationship with him. And although Christ himself tells us to 'Ask, and it will be given you' (I am looking ahead to Chapter 7, v. 7) he qualifies this in Luke (11:13) by naming the Holy Spirit as the 'good thing' which he will give.

Our quest should be for God, not for earthly treasure. Why are we always trying to cadge gifts from him? Even the reception of the Holy Spirit has been reduced, in some quarters, to 'gifts of the Spirit' alone; but what Jesus himself tells us is to seek the Kingdom of God – that is, to seek to live in God's Presence, to offer the Holy Spirit a permanent dwelling place within our hearts, to contemplate him in reverent love and to pour out the love we receive from him on everyone around us.

Much of the Sermon on the Mount speaks in reciprocal terms – if you behave like this, then God will treat you likewise; because the goal of our faith, a true and living relationship with God, must be a two-way affair. And whereas it is common for people to throw up their hands – rightly – at the thought of ingratiating oneself with God by works, they often fail to see that to demand works from God is exactly the same thing. A union of being and doing on both sides in mutual love is the essence not only of salvation but also of prayer.

The requests of the Lord's Prayer are for necessities: our 'daily bread', spiritual and material, our deliverance from temptation and evil. Later in the chapter Christ will elaborate by telling us that of course the Father has these essential concerns of ours in hand before we have even thought to ask. We make our request not out of real need, nor out of routine politeness, but in acknowledgement that all things come from God and that we are totally reliant on his love and beneficence, in the way that a child confides a trusting hand to a loving Father. We know that his commitment to us is unswerving, whether in fact we ask anything or not.

But the commitment of a relationship is two-sided, and the rest of the Lord's Prayer consists of our commitment to God and our neighbour in equally unswerving self-dedication. The prayer is the establishment of a love-relationship, no more, no less, and whatever way we try to expand it, change it around or use it as a pattern for our spontaneous prayers, that love-relationship must be the essence of everything that passes between us and God. We stand before God and we give our hearts to him in wonder and delight, in response to his sacrificial love for us.

14-24. *Forgiveness and wholeness*

So often we like to think of our salvation in terms of God's assurance already given and received, or dependent on our faith and actions. Rarely do we see it dependent on our ability to forgive. Yet Christ insists on it, repeatedly.

What exactly is forgiveness? How does it relate to pain – to the very real pain we often feel long after we think we have 'forgiven' someone? I can think of two examples in my own life: one involved the injuries I suffered as a result of a car accident. The physical pain remained for a considerable time, and my body is scarred for life. No amount of forgiveness towards the motorist at fault will ever change that.

The second example is of emotional pain, which in one instance continued even though I felt I had fully forgiven the person who had injured me. Taking the physical example as a guide, one can see how pain and the absence of forgiveness are not synonymous. Indeed, they can even be the opposite. I am thinking of Christ on the cross, totally forgiving, yet not only enduring great suffering in body but in spirit also. He was suffering our pain – that is, the pain of his tormentors, the very people he had forgiven.

50

So perhaps we can see through pain to forgiveness, even accept it as a sign of our love and solidarity for the one who has wronged us.

We can see then that the whole question of forgiving and being forgiven is not, as a cursory glance at this text might lead us to believe, one of a legalistic tit for tat attitude, but a relationship of love.

There is nothing like being burgled to bring home the truth of not laying up treasures on earth! Yet still we cling to what we can see with our eyes rather than what the eyes of our heart reveal to us: the beauty of God, the beauty of his words, the beauty of life as it could be lived according to the Gospel.

How divided we are! We not only try to separate our lives into what concerns God and what concerns mammon. We also try to divide up the human person into a spiritual self and a physical. We understand care for the one as of no use to the other. So we have lost the true spiritual dimension of fasting, which is precisely to unite soul and body and to involve our physical nature in our prayer life, and relegated it to the unnecessary, because it belongs to the 'low' side of us. In practice, of course we indulge that 'low' side like mad – witness our constant over-eating and drinking – and we persuade ourselves that is no concern of God's.

Divisiveness – whether of forgiver and forgiven, or body and soul, or material and spiritual – is deadly, Christ warns. Restoration to wholeness in love is the Gospel message, and we ignore it time and again.

25-34. *Focusing on the Kingdom*

We think of anxiety as a modern phenomenon. Stress, depression, mental breakdown are said to be symptomatic of twentieth century living. The Gospel shows us otherwise.

Our problems may be different – not so much the first

century peasant's concern with where the next meal is coming from but the threat of redundancy or the pressures of a high-tech society – but the inward-looking, self-destructive anxiety which they cause is just the same. We shrink the Kingdom to the size of our petty preoccupations.

So: look up! says Christ. Look up at the birds in the sky, look out at the beauty of the landscape, see God manifested in power and glory in the whole cosmos; see the true extent of the Kingdom all around you.

In this vastness it is not we who become small, but our problems. We remain of infinitely more value than the birds or the wild flowers, because what lies deep within each of us, underneath the oppression of our anxieties, is the image of God; and its natural habitat is not the prison of our tiny world of fears and difficulties but the vastness of his Kingdom.

Why am I not worried about my continual pathetic efforts at living outside the Kingdom? Why does my godless anxiety about the humdrum and the secular eclipse my desire for Christ? Why do I not see the Christian struggle as the most pressing – indeed the only – thing worth worrying about?

In fact, Jesus does not tell us to worry about the Kingdom but to seek it. To worry can be a sinister substitute for action. You can worry about being out of work or you can get out and look for a job. You can worry about the ozone hole or you can bin your aerosol spray.

I can worry about being a mediocre Christian or I can make a new start by seeking to do God's will in every single situation, beginning with today. Being outside the Kingdom should compel me to action, not out of craven fear but out of the sheer horror at my idiotic preference for the ways of the world to the ways of God. Moreover I should not only be driven from behind by this horror, but I should be dragged irresistibly forwards by the desirability of the Kingdom. I should be completely captivated by its prospect, simply unable to tolerate anything less.

We can only let go of the things that bind us when we

meet something more powerful or more attractive. So long as I see nothing beyond the horizon of my own needs I cannot lay them aside. But when that horizon melts into the infinity of the Kingdom I am free to reach out and receive the vision as reality. Only in the continuous awareness of Christ's presence will I have the strength to undertake whatever he gives me today. If we gaze into his face, all our petty worries disappear.

Chapter 7

The rock of faith

1-5. *Judging others*

These verses concerning judging speak very personally to me. They remind me of a specific occasion in my life: my first meeting with the man who was to become my spiritual father.

Of the many things about which I felt apprehensive prior to that meeting, not least was the sort of questions I might be asked. What were my motives in coming to see him? What did I believe or not believe? What kind of person was I, what were my faults and sins? I was prepared to give honest answers but I recognised that the process might be very painful, and that I might well be reprimanded or even rejected.

What actually happened took me aback. I was asked no questions at all. Merely a willingness to listen and an acceptance of me in whatever way I cared to reveal myself.

That had a devastating effect. I had expected to be judged, as a prerequisite to being healed. But here was no judgement at all, only an outpouring of love which was totally unexpected. Even as I sat there I could see that this refusal to judge was a principle which I should in gratitude adopt as my own. I was normally so ready to pass sentence on others; it was one of my most obvious failings. Now I could see how godless it was. It must stop.

Alas! Those are easy words to say, and so difficult to put into practice. Yet even if my success has been small I have at least become conscious of the necessity not to judge, and the very deep effect that that can have on others.

So I know with burning conviction how true the words of these verses are. Acted upon, they can turn a life upside down. If we are genuinely Christ's living presence in the world today our vocation is not to judge but to save it. If God has not condemned me but has accepted me in love, how can I dare to treat my neighbour otherwise?

That does not make Christianity a soft option. It does not mean condoning sin or failing to stand up for what is right. But it does mean meeting every person who comes my way where they are, not on the self-righteous pedestal where I habitually am; and not jumping in to criticise and change them but so revealing divine love to them that they cannot help but respond to it.

And the less time I spend picking other people to pieces, the more I will have to put myself to rights.

6-14. *Growing towards God*

I find the juxtaposition of verses 6 and 7 fascinating. We humans are apparently told that God will give us what we ask; but we in our turn are to be very circumspect when it comes to passing on his gifts. What are we to make of this? Are we really to look with supercilious scorn on the profane unbelievers around us, considering them as dogs and swine?

Jesus himself spoke in similar terms to the Canaanite woman, virtually calling her a Gentile dog. Is that honestly the sort of God one could feel able to ask anything from at all? And yet the woman does. She persists beyond the abrasive brush-off, asserting her right to divine mercy even if she is in his eyes the lowest of the low.

In other words, she really asks. She puts everything she's got – including verbal repartee – into her desperate plea for God's loving response. She is ready to accept utter abasement – the abasement of the Gospel, which Christ himself will accept – in order to partake of his merciful blessing. And having accepted that lowest place she is called up higher, to be given her heart's desire, because she has truly fulfiled the conditions of the Kingdom.

Most of the time we do not. I do not wish to see myself as a dog or a pig. I demand to be called one of God's children. As for asking for 'good things' – how little genuine feeling I put into asking for the virtues of the Beatitudes, and how much into selfish worldly requests! How can God make any sense of that attitude, let alone comply with it? Do I not define myself as a dog by my godless behaviour?

I know the dangers of indiscriminate scattering of what is holy. Are there not times when the innermost experiences of a Christian should be kept within the Church? We can all have moments of extremely personal communion with the Lord which it would be totally inappropriate to bandy about in public. I am thinking, too, of the pain of seeing a television spoof of the Last Supper. If that is all some people can make of the Gospel perhaps it is better for them not to know rather than drown in their own blasphemy.

Even such people can grow, given the right conditions. It is possible for all of us to progress beyond the attitude of dogs to that of children. But God in his infinite mercy knows how to give us not just what we ask, but the right dose at the right time.

He offers us a narrow gate which he knows how to open slowly, giving us just enough of a tantalizing glimpse into the Kingdom to want more. He beckons us seductively. He does not compel us but he does invite us by keeping his treasure on the far side of the threshold rather than throwing it at our feet.

There is a lesson in that for our own attempts at evangelisation.

15-20. *False prophets*

False prophets have arisen down the ages; one has only to think of the various heresies in Christian history, and their originators.

What of today? I am not really thinking about secular 'prophets' of materialism, promiscuity and so forth, much as they bedevil our lives, but those within the broadly Christian framework whom one could consider the perpetrators of all kinds of false ideas. I would personally include liberal demythologisers and 'Success Gospel' tele-evangelists among those who distort the Christian message into something almost unrecognisable.

It is not, of course, a question of whom we humans see as a false prophet which matters, but God's opinion! We can very well be blinded by our own bigotry, and there are bigots enough in every church and Christian grouping. Yet we do need to discern – Jesus tells us in this passage – who are the false prophets, in order not to be led astray by them.

He gives us the criterion. What results do they achieve? We are to look at what they do and what they are. Have they truly become mouthpieces of God – and do they live their message, his message?

Ultimately we have Christ's comforting word that they will not prevail, but in the meantime we must be on our guard.

So far, so good. But what of myself? Do my fruits give the lie to every 'pious' word I say or write? What are my fruits? They should be synonymous with my message; I should be a walking Gospel. Can I be sufficiently wounded by that thought, today, to goad myself into a change of heart, so that like John the Baptist I can truly become a voice embodying God's word in the desolate wilderness of modern society?

21-29. *Judging ourselves*

Jesus paints a picture of the Last Judgement in which he confronts many apparent Christians who thought they had fulfilled his work in his name; and he rejects them as strangers and evildoers, because he says that in reality they had been acting according to their own will and not God's.

How far does this apply to me? How often can I honestly say I know what the precise will of God is, let alone fulfil it? I muddle on; most of the time I avoid doing anything very much, and when I am faced with action I am too little attuned to God to know what to do or say in his name.

Can we imagine anything more devastating than to come face to face with our Lord Jesus Christ, whom we profess to love, whom we long to see, to be in his shining presence for all eternity – only to be rejected by him? Is the desire to hear his voice – the desire of my life – to be fulfiled by words of total, eternal damnation?

This dread possibility is truly the most terrifying thing, and Christ repeats the warning throughout his ministry. The Parable of the Sheep and the Goats speaks the same dire message: judgement will be for some – for 'many' he says here, even for those who were confidently anticipating the opposite – utter, irremediable rejection.

What we see revealed here is no appeal to faith, no appeal to works; no expected spark of recognition or mercy in the Lord's eye: just a compelling honesty, as all that is only apparent, all that is tainted with the Lie, is uprooted and cast out from the perfection and truth of eternity.

'Thy will be done.' All our salvation seems to hinge on these words, which we repeat so lightly day by day. We should not content ourselves with belief in God at a distance but stand before him daily eagerly awaiting his orders, delighting to join our will to his and to fulfil it by all our works.

That is the theory. Do I honestly put it into practice? How often do I complain that God has not revealed his will for me, and then when he does I take it not as a word to be embodied and lived out but a possible course of action which, according to my God-given human freedom I may accept or reject, more or less with impunity? 'Thank you, Lord, for showing me what I ought to think or do. Today I will consider it, and will possibly choose to do otherwise.' Sometimes those words are uttered with despair or regret, but at other times with callous indifference to the Crucified.

Only in rare pious moments do we want to be slaves to the divine will. (And as a rule we are much more comfortable with the translation 'servant'.) The rest of the time I struggle to preserve my cherished independence, and self-interest, and I cover this all up with lip-service prayer, self-enhancing actions of my own choosing and a distorted faith in God's indulgence towards my wilful disobedience as if it were an endearing foible.

So these words of Christ's are there to hit us sharply. Yes, there will be judgement, but it begins today, with ourselves. We can come to our senses now, and put things right. We can tear ourselves away from this sham of a Christian which we are and begin again in sincerity. We can condemn the old Adam in us and grow into the new Adam, the measure of the stature of the fullness of Christ.

I believe that if we judge ourselves in that way, then at the end of time when we come as sincere but knowingly unprofitable slaves having scarcely done our duty, we will see the light of Christ's glory as radiant mercy, as it truly is, and not as the burning fire of condemnation. We will be capable of joining our sacrificial, self-giving love to his love. We will see our humanity joined to his perfect humanity for all eternity. But all that can only be ours if we can judge and eradicate our dishonest self-righteousness here and now.

Part 3

DISCIPLESHIP

Chapter 8

Faith in action

1-4. Healing the leper

This story is one of those brief glimpses of Jesus healing an
anonymous individual who happens to be in the right place
at the right time. We do not know how contrived that
'happened' was; the leper may have walked for days for
this chance of a cure, or he may simply have been the local
outcast. All we can say for certain is that whatever the
outward circumstances, the meeting was according to the
divine will.

Several things I notice about this incident. First, the
leper comes and kneels before Jesus. Many others did the
same, acknowledging his greatness, his authority – and
their own lowliness. The leper's words also show this
master/slave relationship; he addresses Jesus as 'Lord' and
does not demand, or even directly ask, for healing. He
states his faith in Christ – 'You can make me clean' – and
his reliance on his will. He does not try to impose his own
will on Jesus, as so many of our prayers do.

This evokes the beautiful response: 'I will; be clean.'
And just as in Genesis God spoke and things were, so here
he speaks and the leprosy is cleansed. There is a parallel in
the word Christ will speak to calm the storm; and the word
the centurion will ask of him.

This little passage, then brings encouragement to us. It
is a picture of perfect faith and trust, and God's ready
response; oh, so heartening.

But it also brings to my mind a chilling image. One day
in different circumstances a very similar thing will happen.

A young man will fall on his knees in faith and trust and seek God's mercy. He too will speak in the same terms of submission to the divine will. As Jesus stands here with the leper at his feet does he have any intimation that in the Garden of Gethsemane he himself will be on his knees uttering the words, 'Not my will, but Thine'? Jesus, the Lord and Master of this passage, will ultimately be rejected by the people like this leper. He will be the outcast of humanity, carrying the sores of all our sinfulness. And he will find himself in this leper's place, the place of the sinner, the servant, the beggar, on his knees.

We cannot compare the outcome of the two incidents. Christ, in submitting totally to the Father, accepts not deliverance but death. But what we can ponder, in both passages, is our own response. When I say, 'Lord, if you will', don't I really wish God to conform his will to mine? Do I not always want to be the healed leper, and not the Son of Man in the Garden? Am I not ready, like the disciples, to run for cover as soon as the will of God threatens my skin?

I believe we must return to these questions again and again, because fair weather Christianity is a dangerous vehicle of Satan. Your will be done, Lord – even if it is not mine! Give me strength not to wish always to opt out of misfortune, but when necessary to share in it in solidarity with you and my less fortunate brothers and sisters.

5-13. The centurion's servant

Jesus is confronted by an outsider; a representative of the hated occupying power, a man of war, who should have very little to say to the Prince of Peace.

What does he say? Nothing religious, no declaration of faith. Just a heartfelt plea and a simple statement.

But one so full of humanity. 'Lord, my slave is lying paralysed at home, in terrible distress.' He could have seen this slave merely as a useless possession that must earn its keep or be thrown out – not a human being at all. He could have sought his healing merely on those terms.

What he sees instead is a person in dreadful suffering. His heart goes out to him in sympathy, and it is this sympathy – a word which literally means 'suffering with' – which he brings to Christ.

The Gospel message of the Kingdom is one of participation. We are to share eternal life, with God and with our neighbour; we are to eat and drink at Christ's communal Table; we are to rise with him to become 'partakers of the divine nature' as St Peter puts it. But all this is dependent on our sharing his baptism of death to sin and his path to Calvary. The sharing of suffering is a sine qua non of the Christian life.

This the centurion understands, not intellectually, not by studying theology, but by experience. By relating in love to his servant's pain he can relate to the love of Christ; thus his faith and his awareness of unworthiness are bound up with participation in the Kingdom conditions.

Here is no stereotype Roman soldier but a man of sensitivity who sees with the eyes of the heart what the religiously focused miss completely. Jesus commends his faith; but what prompts it, if not his compassion? In a word, isn't there something Christ-like about him?

And is that not the essence of what we call faith: a bond of participation in Christ's love?

14-22. Taking on

This passage divides into two complementary parts. In the first we see in a comforting domestic setting Jesus the healer, full of tender compassion, responding in love to all who come to him. In the second we see him as the Son of Man, isolated from society and making stern demands on his followers.

In both we see his authority; to drive out evil and disease with a word, to restore to wholeness with a touch, but also to direct men to action. He gives orders to cross the Sea of Galilee, in a tone of voice to which people respond obediently. He speaks out clearly to those who think they can butter him up with pious words; the Word of God is not for the faint-hearted. He issues a challenge which is uncompromising. In everything he is decisive and convincing.

There is another unifying element to these two incidents. It would be easy to think that the first is a matter of Christ's giving: giving wholeness, healing, hope and compassion. That is not how the quotation from Isaiah puts it. 'He took our infirmities and bore our diseases.' All this healing and love was not some bounty he dished out freely, at no cost to himself. He took on all the pain and imperfection and sin, in order to restore all things. Everything was self-sacrifice.

That is the only sort of love which Christianity knows. All too often we are caught out by the sentimental Baby in the Manger, or Jesus cuddling the little children, and we are tempted to think our Christian love consists only in that sort of emotional response. Like the scribe we see the beauty, the goodness, the hope and the joy and we want our share of it. We genuinely want to serve the God who gives.

The God who takes is another matter. Do we really want to give of ourselves, and then in turn learn to take on in sacrificial love in his name all the world's pain? Do we want to leave the comfort of Peter's domesticity and set out across the treacherous sea following an uncompromising Teacher on a journey to Calvary?

If we stop and think, plenty of excuses spring to mind. Some of them seem justified, even religiously worthy. But they are still excuses. I am very conscious in my own life how often I fail to make a distinction between a reason and an excuse.

God will accept them – and simply leave us to get on with things as he goes on his way. The salvation of the world cannot go into suspended animation while I dither. Christ and his work will go forward without me, I am not indispensable to it. There may well be moments in my life when, even though I call myself a disciple like the man in verse 21, I shall be left standing on the shore, too bound up with my own concerns or simply too frightened at present to venture across the lake.

Sooner or later the Lord will pass by and call again. In his mercy he returns to knock at the door of my soul year in, year out, waiting for me to drop everything and respond totally. And whatever I drop he will pick up, take on and bear, even to the Cross.

23-27. *Lord of the storm*

The incident of Jesus quelling the storm threatens modern thinking just as much as the storm threatened the disciples. It arouses in us doubts and anxieties. Will we be derided for taking it literally, indeed can we take it literally? And if so, what kind of picture does it paint of Jesus and his relation to the natural world, not only in Galilee but today, when physical disasters are still one of the great stumbling blocks to belief in a benign God?

How often do we seem to find Christ asleep when we call upon him to rescue us from dangers? Only we cannot literally wake him up. We cannot seem to make him hear no matter how hard we cry out. So either physically or emotionally the wind and the waves overwhelm us, and we drown. And I am thinking not only of our own small problems but of the African starving to death or the earthquake victim buried alive.

Whereas the disciples, who knew Jesus at first only in his humanity, were prompted to ask just what sort of a man this was, we who have already known and trusted him as God may ask just what sort of a god he is, when he appears to remain asleep while we perish. I have been down that painful road myself. The question of apparently unanswered prayer in the face of mindless suffering is one we all have to face in our Christian life – perhaps the sooner the better.

Suffering can be a way we join ourselves to Christ and

participate in his passion; and this can kindle our awareness to the fact that he is indeed awake and beside us, participating in our suffering. That is a far cry from our customary demands and indignation when like the disciples our concern for our own skins blots out our experience of Christ our saving Master. If the latter is true, all our fears are truly superfluous. Yet it is a hard thing to learn.

The contrast to the violence of the storm, the storm in the hearts of the disciples, and Christ at peace, unmoved by the turmoil of the world, is surely the key to the whole episode. Here we see not a man impervious to human concerns, nor a god who is detached and safely out of reach in an impassable heaven. Here we see God become Man, involved, sharing our dangers but remaining above them in control, with the power to project his eternal peace on all things. We see the cosmos respond to the Word, as if it had been given us to take a peep at the Creation. We share with Christ and the disciples a moment of the divine dynamism – a moment which we can use to sustain us when our own turn to cry 'Save, Lord' comes, as it surely will.

It is a moment of the Kingdom, a moment in which we catch a glimpse of the perfect harmony, perfect peace, perfect oneness of God with his world. It is a moment in which we are included in this oneness.

All miracles are such moments of the Kingdom. So, too should be our times of prayer, times of worship, times of giving of self to the Lord; times when we find ourselves face to face with the peace and power and majesty of God in an experience of real strength to be stored to carry us through the bleak times. Christ is the Lord of all things, as we have surely witnessed powerfully at times when the veil has been lifted and we have truly participated vibrantly in the Kingdom. We have heard him quell the storm with a word and spread out his peace with a wave of his hand. We know his power has destroyed death, that the Kingdom is ours, that we have risen from the waters of baptism with the storm behind us and eternal calm ours for the taking in faith.

So we have the power to face the mortal storms of life without any fear of spiritual perishing because Christ has already accomplished our salvation.

28-34. *The Gadarene swine*

This is not my favourite version of the Gadarene swine story. I love Mark's description of Legion sitting 'clothed and in his right mind', a beautiful picture of wholeness restored to this victim of fragmentation.

What we see here is the fragmentation made ultimate. 'Legion' is presented as two different people, perhaps the tearing apart of an individual. The internal dividedness of humanity is our basic fallen state. This is what we die of as our souls and bodies are wrenched apart as objectively as Legion's. This is what Christ has come to restore, and here we see the process at work; a promise, like the raising of Lazarus, of our final restoration in resurrection, and the ultimate destruction of evil.

The cry, 'What have you to do with us, O Son of God?' is very close to Christ's own words to his mother at the wedding of Cana.

'What is your relationship with me? One of power? Are you here to control me, tell me what to do?' All this seems to be implied in this phrase.

Christ truly does have power and authority over evil spirits. His word to them is 'Go'. It is in contrast to his mother's reaction. Even as his physical mother she does not have power over him. She aligns herself with the servants: 'Do whatever he tells you.' She joins her own will to the will of her Son.

How often do I ask him affrontedly what rights he has over me? And how often does my behaviour cause him to ask me what rights I think I have over him?

Do I not try to make God my servant, a God in my pocket who will do my bidding whenever I call on him? Do I ever in my arrogance stop to hear him asking me this damning question, and do I ever hear the words of his mother, addressed to all those of us who claim to be his servants: 'Do whatever he tells you – not the other way round'?

It is easy to see these demoniacs as people far removed from myself. I know what schizophrenics are, I am not aware of such brokenness within myself either mentally or spiritually. Like the Gadarenes I do not think I need healing; indeed, the possibility is a threat. Things are ticking over quite nicely as they are, I do not want the intrusion of anything to disturb my material well-being.

I once heard a beautiful sermon on this passage which pointed out that Christ made the crossing of the Sea of Galilee, endured the storm, endured the rejection of the Gadarene people solely to heal these outcasts. Not one of us, however far we have travelled down the miserable road of spiritual hostility, spiritual madness, spiritual fragmentation, is irredeemable. Even if I have no awareness of my own need, he will cross oceans to find me.

Chapter 9

The depth of response

1-8. *Freeing the paralytic*

The account of the paralytic healed in Christ's house reveals something very important about the nature of faith. Mark and Luke include the detail of how the sick man was let down through a hole in the roof made by his friends in their frantic effort to bring him into Jesus' presence.

Christ responds to their concern. The Gospel puts it, 'when Jesus saw their faith' – not just the faith of the invalid but the faith of his friends, too. In this context the word 'faith' is much more than belief in Jesus, wider even than trust in his goodness and power. It includes the men's concern for the paralytic and the confidence that it is shared by Christ. How otherwise could they have dared to demolish the roof of his house?

There is another point here: the concern of Christ for the whole person of the paralytic. He healed him body and soul – indeed, he makes it quite clear that far from being two separate entities body and soul are intertwined, they equally make up the one unique being which is the human person.

How beautiful it is to see that we are not merely a soul lodging for a season in an inferior and 'not quite nice' body as the pagans reasoned but that we are a unique wholeness, communing to the divine in our spirits, communing to the material world in our bodies. All through the Gospel this is made clear as Jesus combines healing and teaching in his ministry, as he concerns himself with both physical and spiritual needs. Finally in his own bodily resurrection, when he takes the matter of this world into eternity; as he sanctifies us body and soul through the material substances of bread and wine; as he promises to us also resurrection in body and soul and, indeed the renewal of all creation, we are assured of God's hallowing of matter.

We may see faith and love as spiritual things, but it is only with our physical selves that we can put them into practice. This is exactly what the friends of the paralytic had discovered. They had to transform their faith in Christ and love for their friend into practical action. They had to use their muscles as well as their hearts. They had to work as the unique creatures they were, the mysterious union of soul and body which is humanity.

That is precisely what Christ healed; not sins and legs separately, but the whole person.

9-13. Respond!

Jesus' eating with tax collectors and sinners highlights his respect for even the lowest people. But he does not just respect us, and leave it at that. He offers us healing. He refers to himself as a physician. Yet while many people are physicians, what is incredible about Christ is that he heals the unhealable – all those things, whether diseases, mental attitudes or sinfulness – which are totally beyond human healing.

Indeed his very call is healing. Being in his presence does not just create wholeness; it is wholeness. When we stand in the light, darkness no longer exists.

That was Matthew's own experience. Christ simply saw him, said 'Follow Me' – and Matthew did not hesitate.

'And he rose and followed him.' I am reminded of the word once spoken to me by my spiritual father: 'Respond!' And it cannot be written without the exclamation mark. That is how it was uttered, with exuberance, with joy, with invitation. That is how our response to Christ must be when he calls us: free, not an 'ought', but given with love, joy and one's whole heart.

To most modern Christians the practice of fasting is outmoded and irrelevant – even, perhaps, against the spirit of the Gospel; and they cite this passage to support them.

How wrong! Christ is talking here of a specific situation: that of himself and his disciples, for whom the Kingdom has indeed come because God Incarnate dwells in their midst. Does not Christ describe the Kingdom as a feast? In his presence fasting is impossible.

But he rightly warns John's disciples that things will change. In the days when the Bridegroom is taken away Jesus' disciples will certainly fast. Can one imagine them returning home after the crucifixion to sit down to a hearty meal? And how can we on the day of the crucifixion – every Friday – eat and drink, forgetting the Lord's passion as if it were just another day? If we do, then we have no right to talk of Sunday as being the Lord's Day, for we cannot celebrate the Resurrection if we are not prepared to share the crucifixion.

Jesus has already made it quite plain what should be the Christian attitude to fasting. 'When you fast, do not look dismal, like the hypocrites' (Mt 6:16-18). He does not say 'if you fast'; he expects us to fast.

Why do John's disciples fast? Because they are keeping the Law of Moses, given by God himself. It is the call to perfection – 'Do this and you shall live' as Jesus tells the lawyer who knows the Law (Lk 10:28).

But no one in practice reaches perfection under the Old Covenant. Christ, who is himself Perfection, the embodiment of the Law, gives us the New Covenant, in which the Mosaic regulations take on new meaning. The inauguration of the Church will bring about new patterns of feasting and fasting as Christians celebrate Easter instead of Passover and keep Lent instead of the Jewish fasts. In the time after Pentecost in which we live our fasting is indeed to be undertaken with a new purpose, not as a matter of human approval but as a time of regeneration in the power of the

Holy Spirit. The early Church not only understood but practised this. We have examples in Acts of 'prayer and fasting' being exactly the two sides of the same coin as Christ himself described (see Acts 13:3 and 14:23) and St Paul's likening of the Christian life to the disciplined life of the athlete – a total training of soul and body.

For those who think this is dispensable, a word of warning. Today people continue to 'fast', but for just the wrong reasons condemned by Christ in Chapter 6. They diet to make themselves better-looking or to be virtuously health-conscious – in other words, to seek human approval and their own benefit. They take their eating out of the Kingdom and into the realm of secular life, from which they shut God out. They have inadvertently returned to the old wineskins.

If we do not want to make a mockery of the Gospel we must take care not to adjust it according to our own preferences. Christ has not given us licence. He has not made it easy to be perfect. He has spoken simple words, it is true; but they are only simple to keep if we abandon ourselves totally to him. Most of us have not truly taken up our cross to follow him unreservedly to Calvary. So if we are not following in his footsteps, we can hardly claim to be in the presence of the Bridegroom. In that case we should certainly be fasting.

18-26. The fruits of healing

Sandwiched between the account of the raising of Jairus' daughter is the story of the woman with the haemorrhage. All three Gospels recount her words to herself, 'If only I touch his garment, I shall be made well' – words she must have afterwards spoken to others in witness of what had happened. Eusebius tells us her house was preserved and outside it stood a statue of Christ healing her. Her faith bore fruit in her life. If we are healed, we must be prepared to use that healing. Our whole lives must be transformed.

We are back to response. We ask God for healing – or anything else – and we expect, even demand, his response. But then it is our turn to respond; not by a mere perfunctory 'thank you' (and sometimes we don't even manage that) but with our whole lives: with a change of direction, a new beginning.

The deepest response, one person's soul calling to another's, is born of love. When two people are in love they can respond to each other without any overt action, without any word being spoken. It is enough for them to be in each other's presence. Of course, when there is an outward need each will respond, on the deepest but also the most practical level, to that. But the moments of gazing at each other in wondrous silence remain the essence of their communion.

Should that not be our position regarding God? We should be able to respond to him, stand in his presence, out of love and nothing else – and certainly not for what he can, we hope, give us.

27-31. *Enough trust to follow*

What impresses me about this passage is the fact that the two blind men followed Christ as he passed by. 'Followed': a word we hear so often in the Gospel that the significance of it scarcely sinks in here – that to follow someone when you are blind is one of the most difficult things to do. Yet despite their handicap that is exactly what these blind men did – and not just a few steps along the road, but right into the house. They made a supreme effort because for them to follow was a life-or-death matter. Suddenly they had become aware that wholeness was within their grasp and they were determined to go after it with all their strength.

Is that our response to Christ? Do we set our hearts on following him above all else, even when circumstances prevent us from seeing him clearly ahead, when times of hardship or uncertainty leave us in a darkness through which we can only grope our way forward, vaguely aware of a faint disturbance somewhere out there? Is it not rather our inclination to sit tight where we are and lament being left by the wayside, even perhaps to shout angrily to the Lord to drop everything and come to us?

These blind men also shouted, first of all as they followed him outside, and then as they entered the house. Christ did not answer them immediately. They had to be prepared to be persistent, one could say pestering. Their faith had to be stronger than someone who says, 'Let's give it a go' and then gives up at the first sign of failure. No; their faith had to increase with every difficult, halting step they took, it had to be obstinate enough to keep propelling them forward.

And according to their faith they were healed. We are not told what motivated this faith. Was it a question of their 'seeing' in Christ something the sighted people overlooked? They called him 'Lord', they acknowledged his authority, his divine properties. They trusted his power to heal.

How far do I trust the Lord? Do I trust his mercy, his love, his omnipotence, his divine and all-knowing will? Or do I prefer to trust my own judgement of situations, telling him what he ought to be doing? Do I believe in his goodness towards me because I think am a deserving case, to whom misfortunes could not possibly happen? Do I trust myself more than God? If so, I will hardly be prepared to follow him through any darkness. Daylight faith is attractive and easy. Faith to follow in the night, to cry out and to continue even when there is no immediate response, this dogged kind of faith to be drawn into the unknown and the perilous and still believe that Christ is able to do all things – this is our Christian calling.

However hard it is, it ultimately brings us face to face with Christ, to feel the touch of his hand which gives healing and light.

The very first thing those blind men saw was literally the face of Christ. No doubt their desire had been for the ability to see everyday things. What was given them was to look into the eyes of God Incarnate. The vision which their faith had given them became a material reality.

The need for that vision is something far greater than the things we commonly ask of God. Our spiritual blindness shuts us in on ourselves, instead of making us more acute in our other senses as often happens with the physically blind. Lord, help us to follow you out of our pathetic but frightening darkness, towards the light of your presence, in which all things are revealed and restored.

32-38. *The snares of emotion*

The healing of the dumb demoniac provokes interesting reactions. The onlookers divide into two camps. 'The crowds', the eager majority which thronged around this wonder worker, 'marvelled'. Itinerant preachers and miracle-workers they had no doubt seen before; but this one stood out. 'Never was anything like this seen in Israel'. They found Jesus electrifying, amazing, unique.

Contrasted with this enthusiastic and open acceptance we find the response of the Pharisees hostile and cynical. They are eager to turn everything they witness on its head; to call good evil, and the power of God satanic.

So it is easy to equate this open-heartedness of the ordinary people with the 'babes' of 11:25, and the sophisticated aloofness of the Pharisees with the so-called 'wise and understanding'. The crowds of the poor, the sick, the outcasts had perceived the Kingdom, while the religiously self-righteous intellectuals turned their backs.

Naturally, we identify ourselves with the crowds, at least in intention if not in intellect. If I had stood there listening to the Lord, seeing his compassion for the sick turn into concrete healing before my eyes, I could have responded in no other way than to join my voice to the cry, 'Never was anything like this seen in Israel.' I feel I would have shouted it at the top of my lungs, caught up whole-

77

heartedly in the elation surrounding me, much like evangelical fervour at modern mass crusades.

But how does Jesus react to this adulation? He does not detect in these jubilant, excited crowds a deep commitment, only helplessness and confusion. 'Like sheep without a shepherd', Matthew puts it, which should surprise us, because after all here they were in the presence of the Shepherd par excellence. Yes, they were at this moment following his voice; but he was astutely aware that the slightest distraction could send them off in another direction, bleating after a plausible thief.

So, as Matthew changes the simile, Christ likens them to wheat fields awaiting harvest by a righteous lord, but vulnerable to every gale and pestilence so long as the reapers have not yet gathered them.

I see in this a terrible warning. It is easy, as the simile changes, to transfer ourselves from the object to the subject, imagining that we can detach ourselves from the *hoi polloi* and become the reapers already in the Lord's service to bring in the harvest around us. But if we put ourselves back in the crowds for the moment, what I think we ought to discern from this passage is that we too remain vulnerable – indeed, at every hour in mortal danger from being led astray.

And if we think we have no need or right to doubt our salvation given at baptism, taken on when we accepted Christ into our hearts, let us ponder that these simple people were not so dissimilar. Many may have been baptised by Jesus' disciples; many would have responded with all their being to his message of salvation; the whole crowd had been seething with an acceptance as tangible and genuine as any found at a contemporary Gospel rally.

And yet Jesus perceived that all this fervour could be turned. This crowd that would follow him, that would journey with him to the Passover at Jerusalem, would hail him again as he rode in triumph into the city – only to cry 'crucify' a few days later. Mass hysteria is above all something that can be manipulated, and Jesus was painfully aware of the consequences.

So if I am ready to identify myself with this crowd here in the safety of Galilee, where do I see myself in the tragic setting of Jerusalem, when all heads will be turned by the voice of ravaging wolves? Who of those there shouted down the cry of 'crucify'? Not the disciples, not the simple-hearted peasants who had been awestruck by Christ's miracles. None of us can imagine what part we would have played had we been in Jerusalem on that fateful Friday morning, because all the parts are too terrible to contemplate. All we can hope is that we might have resisted the mass hysteria and stayed indoors with our heads down, trying to block our ears to the clamour. To cast ourselves in any more noble role is in all honesty impossible. There was no noble role in humanity's murder of God.

I am writing this as the Lenten journey nears its climax and the Church finds itself once more on that stark road to Calvary. We travel, of course, in the hindsight of the Resurrection, knowing that all the feelings of grief for our sinfulness which well up within us on Good Friday will be dispelled in the tumultuous Easter cry of 'Christ is risen!'

Yet that paschal outpouring of joy, shouted as we stand shoulder to shoulder in our packed church, puts us precisely back among this crowd: one of the fickle multitude, easily caught up in the mood of the moment, too willing to surrender to the blind emotionalism which renders us totally vulnerable in spirit.

We have seen horrendous examples of crowd manipulation in the exploits of the disgraced American tele-evangelists of the last few years. Modern mass marketing techniques have hyped up religion to be the latest 'experience' commodity. And it has particularly targeted the 'harassed and helpless' in the population – the uneducated, the deprived, the desperate.

No, says Christ. Salvation is not just about receiving but about giving. He demands our life, all our obedience, all our dedication to tread the way not of the gullible crowds but the lonely way of the cross, as we follow him to Golgotha. We are not called to remain the corn wavering in the fields, ready to be battered down by any passing squall. We are called instead to the harvest of martyrdom, as a steadfast witness whether in life or in death.

'Be sober, be vigilant', St Peter tells us, because Satan will come as a wolf to devour the unguarded sheep. This vigilant sobriety is worth a thousand moments of ecstatic crowd emotionalism.

Chapter 10

Mission

1-4. The apostles

It says something about the difference between our ways
and the ways of God that Christ entrusted the entire message of salvation to a collection of a dozen peasants. Fishermen, a tax collector, and others about whom we know so
little that we are inclined to wonder if they did anything at
all in establishing the Church: that would hardly be our
choice. All the qualities we expect to find in modern
hierarchs – higher education, theological training, adminis-
trative experience, leadership skills, sheer middle class
confidence – were overlooked in favour of the simple faith
which is so scorned nowadays.

I am not, of course equating 'simple' with 'simple-
minded'. I am thinking of the simplicity of unswerving
discipleship in love and obedience, of total dedication of
self, body, soul and spirit, to God at whatever the cost; total
response to the call to leave everything and follow Christ.
Nevertheless it does cut right across what we consider as
necessary qualifications for the priesthood.

They would be filled, of course, by the Holy Spirit. Here
in this passage, before Pentecost they were potential but
not fulfilled men. However, they were already mature
enough for Christ to send them out with authority of a kind
rarely admitted by today's prelates.

What do we think of these Apostles of whom we know
so little? We tend to forget that the others gave their lives
just as completely for their faith as Peter and Paul, with the
humility of people who were content not to receive any

worldly glory from it. Exactly what their individual part was in building the Church is known not to us but to God, and it is he who will seat them on thrones judging the tribes of Israel, as Christ himself tells us.

What of Judas? He is included in the authority imparted by Jesus, he is given the name of apostle with the others. How frightening! The tare is allowed to grow alongside the wheat, even nurtured lovingly with it and given the freedom to wreak its own bloody harvest. That is not how we humans would have arranged things, either.

When we think about the saying, 'My thoughts are not your thoughts, neither are your ways my ways', do we not tend to think of God's thoughts and ways as being far above us not only in remoteness but also in wisdom? We forget that this 'wisdom' very often appears foolish to us.

We should be more ready than we are to accept God's foolishness. We can see with hindsight the achievements of the Apostles but only God has hindsight in our present situations. Here and now the Kingdom is still at hand, restoration and wholeness can still be ours, free, together with Satan's tares proclaiming worldly wisdom for the price of thirty pieces of silver. But we live in the time after Pentecost, with the Holy Spirit to lead us into discernment and all truth.

5-15. *Accepting God's peace*

The Apostles, sent out on a mission, are among other things to seek out the worthy and bring peace.

We hear the words in the Eucharist, 'Peace be with you', as a routine blessing. But I suspect what we often harassed Christians hope for is not just God's blessing but a share in his inner serenity, to blot out our modern psychological turmoil. Is that what we receive in the Eucharist? Is that what the Lord delegates the Apostles to impart?

And the peace is to return from those who are unworthy.

Does this imply that our own failure to retain God's peace stems from our unworthiness?

The command to shake the dust off their feet is such a practical a piece of advice! 'Don't dwell on what hasn't worked out, put it firmly behind you and go on to the next thing', the Lord seems to be saying.

Yet it also has a more serious meaning: a ritual gesture of condemnation, the reverse of giving the peace.

The frightening thought is the possibility of that being applied to us. Do we ever so refuse to receive God or his peace that he shakes the dust off his feet against us? Do we see him receding into the distance, his face resolutely set towards someone more receptive? And why not? Are we really so utterly worthy, or are we blinded by the dust in our eyes?

16-23. Endure to the end

This clear picture which Christ gives us of the sheep sent out among wolves is not a warning but a promise. 'You will be hated by all for my name's sake.'

We have seen that happening in Russia during the years of Soviet rule. Children have literally delivered up their parents, and brother brother – that was expected 'virtue' in the days of Stalin's reign of terror, just as it was in the Roman Empire.

Yet most people nowadays read this passage and pass over it lightly as something far removed from themselves. The worst that happens is a little ridicule now and again. But I am convinced we have to keep the mentality of preparedness and willingness for persecution; of worldly opposition as the norm.

'But he who endures to the end will be saved.' When we are faced with the ultimate test of our faith, the Holy Spirit will speak for us; not perhaps to save our skins – we can think of Stephen – but to perfect us in our witness. What follows will be his will, which we can accept with boldness and joy.

24-31. God in control

'A disciple is not above his teacher, nor a slave above his master.' How often do we tend to think otherwise! We do not expect to be crucified for proclaiming Christianity; in fact the opposite – an enthusiastic reception, approval, admiration, respect, public acceptance. Yet, 'How much more will they malign those of his household!' (verse 25).

And the next word is 'so'; 'so have no fear of them'. It speaks of nothing less than a victory already won; Christ's victory, the Resurrection, won at the price of victorious Calvary – but also ours. It is to Jesus a foregone conclusion that we share both his crucifixion and Resurrection.

These verses show the inseparable nature of the crucifixion and Resurrection, for us as for Christ. Just as we cannot be reborn without first dying to our old selves, so we cannot participate in the Christian triumph without being prepared to share the dangers and trials of taking up our cross. Christ called the crucifixion his glorification, and that is the only glory that we should expect.

'Nothing is covered that will not be revealed.' Nothing Christian will be buried without rising; the darkness of the tomb will be broken by the light of Easter Sunday. But we cannot escape the inevitable progression. We *will* be maligned, persecuted, even murdered; we *will* have to face crucifixion, if we are true disciples. But we face it with hindsight, illumined by the light of the Risen Son.

'Are not two sparrows sold for a penny? And not one falls to the ground without your Father's will. But even the hairs of your head are numbered.' These are beautiful words. Nevertheless the sparrows do fall. God is with us in our downs as well as our ups, but he appoints both. He is not just aware of our lives, but in charge of them.

I see in this great encouragement. Our misfortunes, our tragedies, our disasters – even disasters in our inner spiritual life and Christian ministry – are in the hand of God. There is nothing to fear. We rest certain in the Resurrection

triumph. He is ultimately in control, despite appearances –
so we can accept them with equilibrium.

And of course when we are in the thick of it that is very
hard to do. Nevertheless, that is Christianity. That is what
should mark us out, as people who are prepared for any
rebuff, any persecution, any hatred from the world;
because the Resurrection is a fait accompli.

32-42. Living God's love

There is a danger in forgetting the context of these
verses. Christ is talking specifically to the Twelve before
sending them out on a mission. He has been warning (or
promising!) them of the dangers they will encounter. Here
he spells out the ultimate reward they will receive. Yes,
there will be justice for the faithful.

Verse 37 talks about the person who loves family more
than Christ. All love emanates from God; it cannot exist
apart from him. Yet often it is appropriated by humans for
their own selfish ends. It remains love of a sort, and therefore a godly thing. Nevertheless, if God is not a conscious
part of the loving then it becomes something smaller than it
could be; it loses a spark.

It we first love God, then the new perspective in which we
live will change our whole existence and we will then
transform the love we have for our families into a higher state
of love. Overflowing with love for God, our response to the
glorious realisation of his love for us, we will not be able to
restrain ourselves from bursting with love for our families in
a far greater intensity than was previously ours. If, however
our normal human love is all that we have, then we will have
fallen short of our vocation as Christians to radiate divine
love; we are not worthy of God or of bearing his name. It is
not a question of God's seeking our affections jealously but
of wanting to bestow on us, and through us to all people, his
own love which is infinitely more splendid than any feelings
we may have on the purely human level.

Christ does not intend to set us against each other in hatred. He has certainly come to upset the tables of the money-changers, to disturb the peace of the ungodly and evil. Satan has to be conquered. But we are also, as Christians, to be peacemakers, called to bestow peace on those who respond to God, as we saw earlier in the chapter.

In short, in our Christian life we will meet opposition and conflict, in which it is our function to bring Christ into the situation come what may and at whatever cost to ourselves – and the cost is ultimately the Cross. But by putting human considerations behind our concentration in love on God, we will then have our whole lives truly in focus. All the rest will then be added unto us.

Chapter 11

Seeing and believing

1-15. *Face to face with Christ*

The messengers from John the Baptist come to Christ to ask a straight question, and what they receive is not, as they probably hoped, a straight answer but a statement almost in the vein of the Delphic oracle: make what you will of it...

It seems to me that this reply – take back to John the evidence which you yourselves have witnessed – is so much better than a bald 'yes'. On the one hand it says, 'listen to the evidence, weigh things up, draw your own conclusions; don't take my word for it but think for yourself.' It is an invitation to look into what John knows of Jesus and events and to use his integrity to take his own decision.

On the other, it says, 'look, if I merely said "yes" you would be able to reply "how can I believe? Where is the proof?" But instead I offer you the proof, so that you may have no doubts. You don't have to take my word for it only."'

I am reminded of the people who heard the Samaritan woman talk about Christ. When they met him themselves they were able to say, 'Now we believe, not just because of what you said, but because of our own experience.'

This experiential knowledge of God is the key to faith. It does not have to be an experience which is dramatic, like a miracle or a sudden revelation or a voice from heaven; but we must be able to say, sooner or later, I know God; I know God because I have met him. However distantly or fleetingly or vaguely, we must have had that experience of

87

a relationship, so that we can join with the writer of Hebrews in saying that our faith is the certainty of things unseen.

Yet poor John, who had grown up with Christ, who was his cousin, who had know him in everyday situations and acknowledged his holiness at his baptism – even he, imprisoned, perhaps caught off guard by his debilitating and demoralizing predicament, was assailed by doubts. John's whole life had been lived not only in the presence of Christ but dedicated to his advancement as the friend of the Bridegroom, prepared to let his own star wane in order for Christ's glory to shine. And suddenly, standing on the brink of death, he is overcome by the terrifying possibility that everything he had lived for and was about to die for might be false.

Here is a timely reminder that the tragic circumstances of human life – often physical hardships which have no immediate 'religious' connotations – can wear down even the most convinced person. We can keep this in mind for our own times of trial.

So often we think that if only we could come face to face with Jesus, all problems of disbelief would disappear. His divinity would be so obvious. But as this passage shows, the cares of the world can cast a veil over the eyes of the best of us – not to mention the majority, who cast the veil so convincingly over their own eyes. Thousands met Christ and saw in him nothing but a man who made preposterous claims they could not accept. Lord, help us to see!

16-19. Walking beside him

Jesus compares the public around him to perverse children sitting in the market place. Whatever the people heard, they refused to respond. They condemned John the Baptist for being an ascetic and then they condemned Christ for not being an ascetic! You just can't please some people; they always find excuses.

88

Yet verse 39 shows us that both ways can yield fruit, and the crowds should have seen the fruit – they had both Jesus and John before their eyes, both giving good results, as it were, both holy men. And still the people did not believe. It was no wonder that Christ upbraided them for failing to repent.

How does this impinge on us? It can serve as a reminder that when people around us are not converted it is not necessarily our fault. If both John the Baptist and Christ himself, between them catering for all religious tastes, as it were, left some people cold, then we are certainly going to encounter the same thing. There is so much hardness of heart, so much determination to find an excuse for rejecting Christ. That is exactly what his own generation was doing: looking for excuses, determined to be perverse, determined to ignore the Gospel.

On the other hand, in how many ways do I ignore the Gospel – its daily demands, its ins and outs, which one can always find excuses for not carrying out at this particular moment? 'Seek first the Kingdom, and all these things will be added unto you.' But how often do I seek first my own desires, leaving the Kingdom in reserve for a pious interlude?

This very day I must walk as a citizen of the Kingdom, or at least as a seeker after it. I must walk beside Christ at every minute of the day. As soon as I turn away from him, shut him out while I do something unworthy, I am like the people in this passage – seeking an excuse for not following Christ.

O Lord, come with me into this day; and may I not leave you!

20-26. *The fire of God*

Together with the preceding passage, these verses speak of response; or rather, our lack of it. The people did not respond to John's asceticism. They did not respond to

89

Jesus' more relaxed, festive style – like perverse children intent on not joining in whatever game you played. And now we see that they had not responded to Christ's 'mighty works' – healing, miracles, teaching. The people's hearts remained like stone. They could not be shaken out of their sin, their Godlessness.

And the warning which Christ utters – or is it a promise? – is that this attitude will bring ultimate disaster at the Judgement.

So how can I state so lightly that I have failed, on such and such an occasion, to respond to the Gospel? Is that not the most tragic and damning sin? One tends to think that Christian response requires enthusiasm – which is true. But something deeper is also involved: the much more fundamental and serious business of metanoia, of repentance in its most compelling sense of a complete about turn in life, a setting out in a totally new direction which inevitably leads further and further away from the old self.

And that cannot be done with the measure of half-heartedness which we commonly think suffices but which in practice works continuously to pull us back towards our former direction. There has to be a break, a new start.

Enthusiasm is a wonderful thing but all too often it is short-lived. We may start out on our Christian journey bubbling over with it, but our tendency is to go off the boil, to settle down to an imperceptible simmer. Sheer enthusiasm will cool if not kept alive by a burning repentance; that is the heat on our face as we turn towards the light of the Living God.

This burning heat of the fire of God is something available to everyone who turns Godwards. We do not have to be theologians or worldly wise. Jesus repeatedly calls us back to childhood; that trusting innocence, that abandonment to love which too often we think it clever to grow out of.

I once watched an unbeliever and his young son being introduced to a celebrated preacher. The adult shook hands, listened to his words unmoved and turned away. The little boy simply looked up into the man's face. They caught the twinkle in each other's eyes and exchanged smiles full of love.

A relationship had been established. It was not dependent on intellectual argument but on openness of heart. An open heart will catch sight of the tiniest twinkle. A closed heart will not even see the mighty works performed at Chorazin and Bethsaida.

27-30. Our Lord and Master

In a world without slavery we can no longer comprehend the significance of taking on a yoke. We like to think of ourselves as free agents. But Christ tells us otherwise. We are not to be masterless; we have a Lord. We are to be as slaves – even regarding ourselves as unprofitable ones. We are to humble ourselves as Christ humbled himself. Our life is not our own, but is 'hid with Christ in God', as St Paul puts it.

Again, I believe all these things are not warnings but promises. Are we going to take up the promises? Do I submit to not being my own master, to not being free, to being under orders? Yet what other way is there to live? Lord, today is your day; you have created it – it is fresh from your hands, you have blessed it for my use. How can I respond in any other way than to offer it, and myself in it, back to you in love; to consecrate it to you in wonder and adoration? Because to do otherwise is to live in your absence; in darkness, purposelessness. Lord, I am alert and ready. Give me your orders, and the strength and determination to carry them out.

I do not wear a yoke but I do wear a cross; and 'Whoever would come after me, let him deny himself, and take up his cross, and follow me.' I can remember that each morning as I put on my cross, in an action akin to putting on a yoke. I am not my own; I have been bought with a price.

In front of me today are jobs I would prefer not to do. Yet I can do them as a labour of love – for the Lord; for my family; as a service to the beautiful material world, God's creation. And I can pray as I work. In this way I can be genuinely rested. I can commune with my Master, I can come to know him, if I have truly accepted his cross.

Chapter 12

Kinship, not signs

1-8. *The holiness of God*

The blind legalism of the Pharisees prevented them from sensing the holy which is the source of laws, not subject to them. And Christ himself was holy.

But how easy it is for us to fall into the same trap! Each Church has its pitfalls. Each has rules which should be governed by the first rule of love – that we know – but how often is it easier to be blind to love and to leave the rules to guide us!

Does this not tie up with the story of the Samaritan woman at the well asking about the Temple and receiving the reply that we are to worship 'in Spirit and in truth'? The holy is not enclosed in a Temple of bricks and mortar but in the Temple of the Lord Jesus Christ, the perfect man by whom the Law – and the Sabbath – were given in love; and through him it is enclosed in the temples of our bodies as being at one with his body.

Our response to the holy should be 'mercy', that is, loving-kindness – and not the legalism of seeing God's rule as involving law-breaking and propitiation. If we respond to his love, then our conduct overflows in the same way; petty rule-keeping is swept aside, replaced by an openness to the sense of the holy, our being directed by it, and reflecting it on all around us.

9-13. *The holiness of our neighbour*

The account of the healing of the man with the withered hand reiterates two points from earlier passages: the positive side of the Sabbath, doing good, the Sabbath being for our benefit; and the worth of a person – this time more than a sheep, as Christ puts it. (On the previous occasion he said 'many sparrows'.) The difference is that sparrows, even those sold as caged song-birds as they were in ancient times, cannot have been worth very much. Is it not obvious that we should be worth more? But a sheep had a real market value. Some people in Jesus' time – clapped-out slaves, for instance – might have been worth considerably less.

Do we ever see some people as worthless? Down-and-outs? Lager louts? The Third World masses? Do we not dehumanize whole categories, and devalue them to far below the carcass of a lamb we would buy for the freezer? Do we spend less each week on the starving than on pet food?

We often think that valuing our possessions more than people is a modern philosophy, the product of our materialistic society. This passage reminds us that exactly the same false priorities prevailed in New Testament times. The fault lies in our sinfulness, not in any particular culture.

The people – in verse 14 identified as Pharisees – had put their own price on the man with the withered hand. He was to be their tool whereby they might trap Jesus. They were obviously not interested in the benefit of his healing to him – it was only seen as incriminating evidence against Christ.

What a contrast to the four friends of the paralytic, who brought him to be healed out of faith! Nevertheless, Jesus does not concern himself with the motives of evil men. God is not small-minded; he acts according to what is right, regardless of our machinations. So the Lord is prepared to walk into this trap, because right and love must prevail at all costs – and he was fully aware of the costs.

I am struck again by the Pharisees' hardness of heart.

They witnessed a miracle and they were not overawed like Peter at the draught of fishes, not compelled by the great wonder they had seen to follow Jesus. They came face to face with the might of God and responded with murderous hatred.

That is not what we can ever imagine ourselves doing. It seems absolutely incomprehensible. Did they not at least fear the divine power they had witnessed? Why did they reason that they could destroy him who had raised Jairus's daughter, who had restored wasted flesh before their very eyes?

We always think we are most influenced by what we see. We imagine that problems of unbelief would disappear if God were to appear bodily in front of us. What this passage demonstrates is that hardness of heart in fact has a far greater influence on us than our outward senses. We see only what we want to see, we hear only if our hearts have given us ears tuned to hearing.

We must be careful also to distinguish hardness of heart from the opposite of gullibility. We are not called to be undiscerning. In fact, hardness of heart is itself extremely susceptible – susceptible to anything which will back up its own attitude! Were not the Pharisees pathetically gullible to imagine they could destroy one whose indisputable power they had themselves encountered? Being led by the heart is not the same as being led by the nose. Lord, open our hearts!

14-29. What think ye of Christ?

I once passed a large poster bearing the verse 'What think ye of Christ?' It challenged the occupants of cars and buses as they sped along the street.

What most people seem to think about Christ is nothing at all. They prefer to ignore him completely; he is just an embarrassment.

For the people of New Testament Palestine things were

95

very different. Jesus could hardly be ignored, especially since he posed a threat to some people. My poster's question was being asked everywhere.

The people in this passage had not all made up their minds as they witnessed Christ's miracles of healing at first hand and tried to square his behaviour with Old Testament prophecy. Some were amazed, and wondered about his possible Messiahship. Others had already closed their hearts in opposition and were ready to distort new evidence to fit their own conclusions.

What possible answers were there? The prophet Isaiah had painted a picture of hope – but not perhaps the hope desired by the Jews awaiting liberation from the Romans. Could the crowds see beyond their own yearnings to discern the embodiment of Isaiah's words in the Servant Jesus?

To those open enough he could be recognised in his miracles as the Son of David, the Son of God. But that could be twisted. Call his powers satanic and one had reason to justify his condemnation. If that seems difficult for us to understand we could perhaps think of charlatan 'faith healers' in our own times who feed on the gullibility of the desperate in a demonic way.

Face to face with God Incarnate, the choice was not easy. Perhaps we should be very grateful that Jesus does not literally walk our roads today and compel our attention.

Instead we have these verses, to make of them what we will. We can think of Christ as a healer and miracle-worker. We can think of him as the fulfilment of the Old Testament vision of the Messiah. We can think of him as a figure to be distrusted, someone for whom bogus powers and claims have been made. Or we can see him shining with divinity, bringing the Kingdom to us.

But we must all accept to be challenged by that poster, today. If we put off thinking and seeing until tomorrow we may miss out entirely. 'The Kingdom of God has come upon you', Christ promises; it is not something for us to put aside for the mythical future. The future will be too late.

The whole of the Christian life is summed up in the

word 'today', the eternal now, which is present to us at this moment if we are sufficiently open-hearted – in a promise already, incipiently, fulfilled. Everlasting life is not something beyond the grave; it is here and now superabundance. If Christ has suffused us with the Holy Spirit then the Kingdom has already come; we are its citizens today. Then we will see clearly to discern in the healer of our souls and bodies, and in the words of Scripture, our King and our God, who sets us free from the enemy.

30-37. *Careless words*

Christ warns us that at the Last Judgement we will be judged by every careless word we have uttered.

What a frightening thought! How easy it is to let a heedless word slip out, to cause others untold doubt, misery or anger. The process, Christ explains here, really starts further back, in keeping a guard on our hearts. If we let no evil intrude into the innermost core of our being – not just the mind but the heart – it will be impossible for us to utter an evil word. There will be nothing to slip out because we will only be capable of speaking the good thoughts already formed in our hearts.

That is a very tall order, but one which we are called to make a start on even if we cannot yet perfect it.

The great ascetics of the Church talked constantly of pushing away evil and negative thoughts and replacing them with good and positive ones, as Christ himself tells us in the parable of the seven evil spirits coming to dwell in the house just swept clean. All the time we must strive to walk with the Lord Jesus Christ – thinking, becoming every good thing. If I am aware of his presence with me at each moment, how can I wallow in nasty thoughts? If he is my constant companion I cannot dwell on, or in, evil.

This leads back to the beginning of the passage. If we claim to have the Holy Spirit within us, how can we think and speak evil? It is plainly impossible.

The truth is, for most of us the companionship of Christ and the indwelling of the Holy Spirit are intermittent things, or at least our consciousness of them is intermittent.

We could start by making the most of those times of consciousness. When I remember Christ's presence, when I feel the Spirit breathing within me, then I must surely put every effort into standing blameless before them, opening myself to perfect Good, banishing every evil thought and inclination. Having made this positive start I can move on to increasing my occasions of perception. Times of prayer are obvious ones, but I am thinking also of the awareness of Christ's presence during the day as one goes about one's work and as one meets people and situations which desperately call for the Lord's presence.

One of our Russian saints has said that the awareness of God should be with us like a toothache – something constantly nagging, now in the background, now demanding all our attention, but never letting us rest contentedly.

If we can learn that, real growth will be possible.

38-45. *Grace already given*

If ever there was an evil and adulterous generation, this must be it. The moral fabric of society seems to be crumbling by the hour.

Yet we have only to think back to Nazi Germany to see that it has all happened before. Then there were Stalin's purges, the French Revolution, the horrific persecutions of the Early Church by Imperial Rome – and in the relatively quiet, rural province of first century Judaea, exactly the same, Christ tells us.

Had the people of his day, like us, hit a peak of moral turpitude, or is it simply that to be a sinful and adulterous generation is a pretty constant condition of fallen humanity?

Either way I can see our own society reflected in this passage. Like the carping crowds around him our dialogue with Christ is too often one of arrogance. We demand things of him, we command him to show his hand. We expect him to work wonders for us but when we have received healing we fail to see the need to do anything on our part. His beneficence evokes no response; no guarding of the heart, no attentiveness to his word, no doing of the commandments. And we are affronted when this leaves us vulnerable to worse temptations than we knew before.

This attitude, he tells us, spells terrible danger for us. We have been given the resurrection. Why do we ask for anything more? Doesn't our continuous whining show that we have, in fact downgraded the resurrection as something peripheral to our lives?

If we have failed to treasure the only source of rebirth into newness of life, will we perhaps be enveloped not by the saving waters of baptism but by evil? Divine cleansing, when we fail to act upon it, can leave us so vulnerable.

We cannot accurately compare one historical period with another, one generation's evil with another. All I can do personally as a Christian is to compare the evil and adultery found in my own heart with the pure image of God which I am called to be. Where this image has been sullied and distorted, Christ is willing to come and restore it to its pristine splendour. But then it is up to me to accept his grace and keep his image pure so that I can become by the power of the Holy Spirit his visible presence to everyone around me.

That is something totally positive, like Christ's divine sweeping clean. It must call forth the positive in us, not the negative inaction which we often think we can get away with. I must learn to run with joy after my salvation, not to sit like a cabbage and ask for signs.

46-50. *One of the family*

I have heard some odd interpretations of these verses over the years. One likened Jesus 'disowning' of his mother and brothers in favour of his disciples to his rejection of the old Israel in favour of the new Israel, the Church.

Such an approach is deeply disturbing. First, because it runs contrary to Scripture: we are told clearly in St Luke's Gospel that all generations shall call Mary blessed; God's grace in her was not a transient thing. Indeed, she is clearly pictured in Acts as being at the centre of the newborn Church with the Apostles and Jesus' brothers.

Second, because it accuses Christ of breaking the commandment to honour father and mother, which is obvious blasphemy.

The language of disowning is totally out of place here. Christ did not reject the old Israel but directed his entire ministry towards it, seeking out the lost and commanding the apostles to begin their own ministry in Jerusalem. In the same way he did not reject the Law; he was himself its fulfilment. He worked from the centre out, teaching us to be ever widening the circle of love which is the Kingdom until it encompasses all creation. He comes to gather, to include, to embrace, to restore. The only thing he rejects is Satan's evil.

By contrast it is we humans who are so fond of rejecting. The first century Jewish establishment rejected Jesus, just as the atheist rejects him today; just as we all reject him every time we follow our own desires. It is we who close the door between ourselves and the Lord, and he who relentlessly knocks at it.

What, then of his Mother and brothers? Mary had heard his knock at the Annunciation and had responded to it unreservedly. She was granted to be Jesus' mother precisely because she accepted to do the will of God – not just in the theoretical sense which is often ours, but in the most practical and demanding manner possible. She heard and accepted his Word in such a total, self-giving way that by the descent of the Holy Spirit in a personal Pentecost the Word could become flesh within her.

That does not make Mary any less or more human than the rest of us. She accepts the will of God at the Annunciation but it remains beyond her understanding. 'How can this be?' she asks Gabriel. She comes to Jesus in this incident, again asking to speak. She cannot doubt his divine Sonship but perhaps the form it takes is incomprehensible. But despite her human limitations of understanding she remains totally faithful. She will not leave Christ at his death, as will the apparently faithful adopted family sitting at his feet here; she will stay not only to see a sword pierce his heart but to be pierced herself. And she will still be there at Pentecost, to witness the coming of the Holy Spirit on the apostles to fill them with the divine presence as she had been filled at the Annunciation.

What does this mean for us? That it is possible, as Christ tells us here and as will be demonstrated at the first Pentecost and our own baptism, for every one of us to offer ourselves as Mary did, to so surrender our whole being to him that we can become flesh of his flesh: not just part of his closest family but part of his very Body.

Part 4

PARABLES
AND MIRACLES

Chapter 13

Citizens of the Kingdom

1-23. Sowing and yielding

We do not have to puzzle over the interpretation of the parable of the sower because it has been given by Christ himself. We are called to yield abundantly, and we would like to see ourselves as the good seed of the parable.

I do not think that realistic! At different times we reflect the range of Christ's analogies; perhaps the seed choked by the thorns of materialism is our most common predicament. I am also on specific occasions conscious of being the seed sown in little depth of soil. What happens to my faith when some personal crisis threatens to scorch me? I suddenly feel alone, bereft of God, wondering if he is there at all. All my convictions wither within me.

At such times one has to say no. No, I will not listen to this evil word with which Satan is choking me. I will listen instead to God's word, both in the printed word of Scripture and in recalling all the experience I have had of him over the years, the love I have received from him. And I will remember the dark moment when Christ, too on the cross felt abandoned by God. I will accept to share his crucifixion agony as my own cross, and cry out to him in my dereliction.

Out of this fearful participation in the cross a new resurrection faith can be born. The dung heap can become the most fertile soil if we let it.

However, there is another side to bringing forth the good yield. I do not always know how I am to go about it. I would like to make my faith much more effective, I yearn to use fruitfully my God-given talents but so often the opportunity seems to be lacking or circumstances hinder my attempts. What is one to make of this?

I suspect that in common with most modern people I am looking too much to externals. Dramatic doing is not necessarily the goal of the Christian life. Where is my growth in the inner life, which would radiate outwards if only I encouraged it to flourish? Like the seed in the parable I should burst forth from my kernel, the divine image imprisoned within its fibrous shell should reach out and blossom.

I am reminded of the words of Milton, writing on his blindness: 'They also serve who only stand and wait.' Waiting can be very positive when it is not idleness but a standing to attention like soldiers on duty awaiting our Lord's orders. When they come we must be ready to be obedient. And obedience is something we can learn in the most humdrum situations of life, while we are waiting.

24-43. *The weeds around us*

The parable of the weeds places the Kingdom of heaven firmly in the world; co-existing dangerously with evil, with imperfection, with hostile forces. We saw from the parable of the sower what is liable to happen to the seed of the Kingdom sown among weeds with their natural tendency to grow faster and stronger.

Nevertheless, Christ tells us here, that is the situation in which the world finds itself, as the unfairly advantaged weeds compete with good seed for favourable growing conditions. We all experience that, and the media taunts us with it daily. How we wish sometimes to escape from this sinful milieu and retire to the desert, a monastery or at least the fictitious God-fearing days of the past.

No, says the Lord, you are not going to be relieved of the weeds. You must continue in the thick of them, taking care not to be overrun but also not keeping yourselves so apart as to languish sterile in an arid land removed from the challenge of everyday living. It may be given to the occasional holy hermit to thrive there but for most people such conditions would spell death.

Death not only for us but for the world. To live out the Christian life in a world which, we know too well, is a complex mixture of good and bad, is the only way we can bring the light of salvation to it. And we must always remember that only God can truly recognise the weeds.

Christ gives us the examples of a mustard seed and yeast: both apparently insignificant, but capable of unimaginable growth. And growth is the key word here. The Kingdom is above all dynamic, ever on the move upwards, outwards, ever increasing in size and depth.

Heaven is not a static state, as boring as the death it is meant to replace. It is not a condition of doing nothing, akin to the shadowy nothingness of the grave. No; it is true life, that is eternal growth, an eternal response to Christ's call to draw ever nearer. It is eternal movement, eternal excitement.

And if we are real followers of his it is already within us, as we experience the exciting growth and movement of a journey already begun even in this weed-ridden world.

44-52. *The Kingdom now*

The Kingdom is also, Jesus tells us, like a treasure, a costly pearl, or a net, similes which describe various attributes of the Kingdom: it is worth selling all for, far-reaching in its search for people but ultimately distinguishing good from evil.

What he does not describe is what it is like inside the Kingdom. This is frustrating for us. There is, of course Revelation, which gives in picture-language a vision of heavenly worship around God's throne. We also know from Isaiah of the 'Holy, holy, holy' sung by the angels, and the image of the wedding banquet. But it is still not what our information-conscious age finds very satisfying.

Can we possibly imagine a Kingdom where there is no evil, where every blemish, every nastiness, every Godless characteristic has been cauterised from its inhabitants? Where joy and love and happiness exist in a measure and a quality beyond human understanding? Where all this is summed up in the glorious and holy face of the Lord Jesus Christ, before whom we eternally prostrate in adoration?

Should we want anything – can there be anything – more? I think we would say our loved ones, our Christian family, our fellow wedding guests. Will we not find them and ourselves in a process of eternal growth, of eternally increasing depth, and bound up in the eternal movement of divine love called perichoresis, the divine dance at the heart of the Trinity?

We cannot begin to imagine the wonder of heaven but we can have a real foretaste of it. Just as thousands of ordinary people in first century Palestine did actually look into the face of God himself, see the Kingdom in his very Person, so we can by reading the Gospel, by communing to him in prayer and in the sacraments, see Christ today in the eyes of our heart. That is already the Kingdom, within us first of all as he said himself.

53-58. The sisters of Christ

After the esoteric talk of the Kingdom we are brought down to earth by this little passage, where Christ returns to Nazareth and astounds the townsfolk with his teaching.

Verse 56 jumps out at me. 'Are not all his sisters with us?' Now, there is uncertainty about the exact kinship of these 'sisters'; behind the New Testament Greek is also the meaning 'cousins' or 'kinswomen'. What strikes me is the fact that these close relations, brought up with Jesus, on intimate terms with him as any other family member, have not even come down to us by name. Of his 'brothers' –

James, Joseph, Simon and Judas – we know only of James, who became first Bishop of Jerusalem and was noted for his righteousness and his knees made hard as a camel's by so much praying. The others are just names. But the 'sisters' are not even that – they are anonymous, so incidental that we have all but forgotten them.

Yet they were a part, perhaps a formative part, of our Lord's life; people joined to him, probably by real affection, who were close to him in a totally unassuming way, who were important to him and he to them.

What must it have been like to have been the 'sister' of Christ? To have basked in the reflected glory of his fame at first, then been burdened with the shame of having him condemned as a common criminal and crucified? And his final, bewildering status of the Son of God, risen from the dead and founder of a new – and persecuted – religion? How did simple peasant girls take all this, how were their lives changed? How did they come to terms with the news that this relative with whom they played as children, teased, mothered, loved, envied – in exactly the same way as any other brother or cousin – was really God in the flesh?

Does it matter to us? Yes; because to dismiss them is, I feel another way we make the Incarnation unreal, ghostly, only a semblance of human life. Of course one must not press idle speculation too far; we can never know the answers. But it is important to remember that such questions nevertheless were real, that these 'sisters' with all their perplexity, their problems, their everyday knowledge of the Saviour in a way we cannot know him, were real.

Chapter 14

The depths of faith

1-13. The death of the Baptist

Only a matter of days after the remembrance of the Nativity of St John the Baptist my lectionary gives this passage telling of his death.

A whole life compressed into so short a time! And in reality, into so few years. His teaching, too, has been compressed, into one sentence: 'Repent, for the Kingdom of God is at hand.' Everything about him is pared down to the bone. He is instantly recognisable in icons, not only for his head in his hand but for his unkempt appearance, the wild look about him. He stands out in the Gospel as a compelling figure of strength, ready to put his weight behind his words. Living his message he stands up to Herod and is prepared to pay with his life.

We can only guess at the impact that made on his cousin. At the news of John's death we read that Jesus withdrew to a lonely place. He had witnessed the euphoria of the crowds flocking to the Jordan, he had been part of that himself. Now he was faced with the other side of the coin: persecution unto death. The path which John had made straight before him was to lead to Golgotha.

But time to ponder on that was not to be given. The crowds followed, he healed them, and there immediately followed the Feeding of the Five Thousand.

Is that saying the time of ascetic preparation is past; behold the food of the Kingdom?

14-21. *Feeding the five thousand*

This is the first of the two miracles of multiplication of loaves and fishes: the feeding of the five thousand. That in itself poses problems for some people. Were they really two events, or two accounts of the same event? I wonder how the cynics who tell us that the Early Church doctored Scripture explain such an obvious clanger?

But to accept literally two stories poses another problem. Does this not make Jesus look like some sort of magician, pulling out a well-tried trick from a standard repertoire? We could almost hear such a figure saying, 'Let's do the loaves and fishes again, that went down well last time.'

The answer must be a closer look at both the Gospel and ourselves. Why am I happy to accept that Christ miraculously healed a succession of blind men and lepers, but not that he performed this particular miracle more than once? I suspect because this one sounds rather less essential and rather more of the repeated set-piece: the same foodstuffs, the same sitting down while Jesus recites 'magic words', the same dramatic collecting up of the leftovers.

And the same compassion. We fix our attention on the material details and ignore the heart of the miracles. Christ has compassion on the people. He is concerned for their bodily needs, whether major ones such as deadly diseases or the everyday such as hunger. He is the God who gives us our daily bread in every sense of the phrase, the God who responds to our ordinary preoccupations as well as our life or death situations.

I see that as a vital lesson to be learnt, just as it was a vital lesson for the people of Galilee, whether they were in a crowd of 5,000 in one location or 4,000 somewhere else. The Good News of the Kingdom which begins now includes God's concern for all our basic needs, and that must be demonstrated just as clearly as his power to raise the dead or forgive sins, because the human person is saved in body as well as soul.

I like the orderliness of this miracle. There is no pushing and shoving to get close to Christ and touch him as there was on other occasions. Instead it has the air of a vast, happy picnic, everyone at ease in the cool of the day. It is almost the King's Banquet lived out on a Galilean hillside – the presence of the Kingdom not in parable, not in the rhetoric of the sermon, not in the tense drama of ultimate need but in the commonplace of a social gathering for a brief moment made perfect as this physical circumstance becomes the bearer of a spiritual meaning.

Just as the smallest of offerings – five loaves and two fish – can be multiplied a thousand-fold in God's hands, so the tiny seed of the Kingdom within each of us can grow if we dedicate ourselves to him.

22-33. *Saved from the depths*

Some modern theologians like to dismiss this passage as fodder for the simple-minded. In reality it speaks such a deep message. There are times when the treacherous sea of life threatens to drown each of us, not only in our worst moments of doubt but even, like Peter, on occasions when we think we are moving God-wards. We hear the Lord say 'Come!' in a way that is compelling, and we respond. Then something happens to shake us – not perhaps loss of faith but a sense of being overwhelmed by circumstances – and we begin to sink.

At that point there is only one thing we can say: 'Lord, save me!' And not in the pious way we commonly speak about salvation but as a real, anguished cry of help. 'Out of the depths I have cried unto thee,' the psalmist says, and that is exactly our experience. At the very moment when we are threatened with being totally submerged, when the tempest outside becomes the tempest within and we drown in our inward fears, we become aware of our need for God – indeed, that no one else can save us.

'Lord, save me!' And Christ, who is never more than an

arm's length away from any one of us, will reach down and pluck us out of the depths, just as in the icon of the Harrowing of Hell he reaches down to Adam and Eve to rescue them from the abyss.

I have felt that arm of his grab hold of me on more than one occasion, and I am aware above all of its strength. It is the powerful arm of the craftsman, sinewy, with a tight grip around one's wrist. What a contrast to the picture the sceptics like to paint of the wimp in the nightshirt performing some unbelievable levitation trick that is only fit for being laughed to scorn by today's thinking person!

No. This is a very real incident: real for Peter finding himself in a life or death predicament, and just as real for us when we find ourselves floundering in the hostile modern world. Christ demonstrates here and in so many situations that he is the Lord, not only of our natural surroundings over which we have no control but also of our human difficulties and problems.

All this I know, not only from reading this Gospel passage but also from my own life. Christ's strong arm is always so obvious in hindsight. But at the moment of submersion it is easy to see nothing but the waves, and become one of little faith!

Lord, you are there to help and support me, awaiting my cry, in every panic situation. You will never let me perish. Stretch down to me, my Jesus, a helping hand and pluck me out from the depths, that I may worship you as God of my salvation.

34-36. What do we expect?

The end of this chapter marks the half-way point in Matthew's Gospel. It prompts me to ask what has my reading done to change my life so far?

Perhaps we should ask ourselves the same question every day. After all, I cannot pretend that I am reading Matthew for the first time. The 'Good News' is not really news for me, it is a well-known story which can never have the surprise impact of totally fresh, unexpected material.

That gives us the unfortunate ability to read it with only half an eye on the page, only half our minds on its significance. Oh yes, the Good Samaritan again, I recognise the familiar words, I know their message backwards – nice to have my memory jogged though, I remember once passing a pub called the Good Samaritan, I wonder if it's still there?

Or should I be saying yes, Christ is calling me with exactly the same words as he did before, giving me the same orders, and what have I done to fulfil them since he last spoke to me?

These short verses also contain the hint of the familiar. Jesus arrives at Gennesaret and the people recognise him. He is not just a name they have heard about. They have seen him before, heard his words before, seen him work miracles before. Like us they are not coming to him absolutely afresh. They know just what to expect.

And look at their expectation! They send around to the whole region. He's here! Come on, everyone, come and receive healing, come and experience his presence, come and be made whole just by being near him!

Is that how I open my Bible every morning? Do I ache to come into the Lord's presence, to reach out and touch even the hem of his garment? Do I just say oh yes, I remember him from last time, and go on my way unimpressed, or do I fight my way up close to him, desperate to be given the chance of a new life of wholeness?

No. I don't feel desperate at all, because I don't really feel sick in the first place. There may be times when I am conscious of being a bit spiritually off-colour, and then it's nice to know there's a bottle of divine aspirin on the shelf, as it were, a well-trusted remedy for life's little ills. But as for real mortal sickness – no, that's not my predicament. I don't need the sort of drastic treatment that will change my life overnight and empower me to get up off my couch of lethargy to follow the Lord. I recognise Christ as a nodding acquaintance, not as my only hope.

We are half-way through the Gospel. We have witnessed Jesus' birth, heard his preaching, seen his power, felt his eyes on us. Now the people of Gennesaret are calling us, inviting us to come closer, to reach out with them, receive healing and follow Christ to Calvary. Somewhere along the way we will have to take up our cross; but only after he has given us the health and strength to do so.

If we can stoop now to touch the hem of his garment it will one day be given us to stoop and see the empty tomb.

Chapter 15

The food of faith

1-20. Faithful to the truth

This passage gives Matthew's version of the Pharisees' questioning of Jesus about his eating with unwashed hands.

I once saw a rabbi demonstrating the Sabbath meal. He explained this hand-washing; a purely ritual gesture, not at all pertaining to everyday hygiene. Of course, he added, if one's hands were physically dirty then one gave them an ordinary wash beforehand.

So that explanation dispels any misgivings we might have about Jesus' eating with dirty hands. No doubt the original Mosaic Law was also concerned with hygiene, at least in divine intention, as well as ritual purity. But not a trace of that was left in the Pharisees' regulations, which were concerned only with the 'religious' aspect.

Of what does religious cleanliness consist? A clean heart, a right spirit, as the psalmist knew. Christ makes it absolutely clear what it is that defiles us in the sight of God. All this is plain to our Christian understanding. Yet there is another aspect to these verses.

We are told that Jesus' words offended the Pharisees. The disciples were moved, in fact, to point it out to him – one feels they were rather embarrassed by their Teacher's outburst against recognised men of authority, despatched specially from Jerusalem to question his untraditional behaviour. They seem to have been uneasy at this clash with 'legitimate' religion, and uneasy also at Christ's harsh words.

We modern Christians may not have qualms about criticising our Church leaders – indeed we make something of a pastime of it in this country – but we are a little more unsure about generally giving offence. Are we not brought up to believe that Christians should be kindly, peaceable people who try not to upset anyone? We know we should stand up for what is right but we are taught to do it in an amenable way. To put people's backs up appears to do more harm than good; instead of reconciling them to God it tends to alienate them further. To offend people is, we feel, rather sinful.

Jesus himself saw fit to use hard words against those who set themselves up as God's enemies. There are times, he says, when the truth has to have a cutting edge, when we need to be angry and abrasive towards the people who perpetuate ungodly lies. We know that we must hate the sin and love the sinner; but there are occasions when that love must be couched in downright ferocity in order to root out evil.

To give offence with just cause is not sinful, because the person whose heart is right will welcome reproof, the Book of Proverbs tells us. We should all be prepared to accept rebuke.

Of course, this does not mean the offence which I give is always right. One's own judgement errs on one's own behalf. But being nice to people all the time at the expense of God's truth is not the bold message of the Gospel.

21-31. Faithfulness and love

This is an interesting follow-on from the preceding passage. Jesus turning his back on the Jerusalem Pharisees takes himself off to a region on the edge of Jewish territory. But he does not collapse with welcome relief into the arms of the Gentiles. Far from it! He reiterates to the Canaanite woman his mission to the Chosen People.

We can make various things of this story. Was Jesus testing the woman's faith by his initial answer, meaning to heal her all along, or did her pleading really change his mind? How does this relate to the subsequent preaching of the Gospel to the Gentiles and its rejection by the House of Israel? The incident provides good ground for speculation, which can become quite a biblical hobby if we are not careful.

What is beyond speculation here is our Christian emphasis on hope. We may always hope, even in situations which look hopeless. 'He that shall endure to the end shall be saved.' We should never be afraid to cry out to God, we should never imagine that we can read his thoughts because first, his thoughts will often take us completely by surprise and second, our ultimate welfare is always his concern, even when outward appearances are contrary.

'O woman, great is your faith!' But in these few verses the woman builds more than faith. She builds a relationship between herself and Christ. She acknowledges him as her Lord, the Jewish Son of David but also her personal Lord even though she is a Gentile. She acknowledges the power of his love – she appeals to his loving-kindness ('mercy'), she places her earthly love for her daughter in the realm of divine love. She indulges in what one might flippantly call banter, but which is in reality the give and take of a real, live relationship with God – not the pious but lifeless prayer which we often offer as a substitute. He is not for her the remote and frightening deity of the Old Testament but Someone with whom she can interact. And interaction is at the heart of a true prayer-relationship with God.

Her faith is no longer the theoretical faith of someone who has heard about Christ from a distance and believes what she hears. It is the vibrant faith of someone who has come face to face with him and entered into a bond of love and faithfulness. Neither will ever forget the other; they are linked for eternity.

Is that how answered prayer changes my life? Or do I simply mark it down as a passing 'success' which I can use as a proof against all the other occasions when my requests are not granted?

I get the impression that, no matter how grateful this

woman was for the healing of her daughter, what really etched itself on her heart was her stunning encounter with Jesus, the Christ of Israel become the Lord of her being.

We do not have to fight our way into his presence as she had to. We are invited by the Lord himself, to his very table, week by week, no longer outcast dogs but children of the New Israel. We are personally called into an eternal relationship with our Saviour. How do we respond?

32-39. Feeding the four thousand

In the feeding of the four thousand we can see the parable of the talents in action. The Lord challenges the disciples, they put their meagre resources at his disposal and find them filled with divine potential.

Something else strikes me, apart from Christ's obvious compassion, his concern for the physical needs of the people: the fact that he gave thanks before he broke the bread.

But the bread was his; as Lord of all created matter he could merely have taken it into his hands and blessed it. Instead he overflowed with love and thanksgiving to his Father. There is thankfulness within the Trinity, together with love – indeed, are they not inseparably linked? When we really love someone, are not our hearts bursting with a constant thanksgiving?

This does not bear any resemblance to the perfunctory 'thank you' we mumble when we are handed something to which we are indifferent. That is not the sort of thanksgiving which should infuse Christianity. Should not everything around us be a cause for thanksgiving, for rejoicing – in short, for expressing our love for God and the recognition of his love for us? And is that not precisely what we see happening here in this passage?

Chapter 16

Taking on

1-4. Asking for signs

The Pharisees and Sadducees come to Jesus to ask him for a sign. His answer is harsh reading. No mention of his 'looking with love' here, as he did to the rich young ruler. Instead he meets tough words with tough words.

That seems to be the only language they understand. They are physically able to witness Christ's gift of healing, his outpouring of superhuman generosity. Yet they are, it seems, blind to all this. They demand a sign, not because they have not seen miracles but because they have failed to recognise divine glory in them. They look into the eyes of God Incarnate and see just a man, moreover a man who is a threat.

He is not behaving like other rabbis. He acts and speaks in a way alien to their own ways.

In all that they were, of course perfectly right. The trouble was, they believed that they were the norm. As the religious establishment of the day they were the ones to whom Christ should defer. Therefore he must prove himself in some unspecified way which will bring him into line with their expectations and their sphere of influence. Otherwise he must remain outside the pale of what they see as their rightful realm. One feels they are certainly hoping that no sign acceptable will be forthcoming. Impervious to divine love, compassion and meekness they want to retain the justification for their hostility.

And divine Love does not turn them away empty-handed. God does not ever force himself on people. Christ, in his divine authority, prophesies his Resurrection. He speaks out starkly in very clear terms on several levels, leaving his opponents to choose which they will hear.

They can catch the note of holy authority in his voice; they can mull over his refusal to call down fire from heaven, as it were, and relate that to the miracles they have already seen him perform; they can meditate on his compassion on the poor and the repentant in contrast to his refusal to be manipulated by their own arrogance; they can ponder what he means by the sign of Jonah, keep it in their hearts for the day when they will hear the Apostles tell of the Resurrection; or they can simply hear their request literally refused, heave a sigh of relief and go home to continue plotting against him.

At this point I am reminded of something I once heard in a sermon on the overturning of the money-changers' tables in the Temple:

'He was angry with them because he loved them.' There is love in this reading, despite the apparently stern tone. Real love shows a deep concern for every aspect of a person's welfare, and that includes having to be severe at times. That is the mettle of a God who faces crucifixion for us.

The Pharisees and Sadducees appeared to receive a rebuff; but it contained all the possibilities I have mentioned. They only had to soften their hearts and they would understand how many signs they had already been given!

What has the Lord given to us, and yet we still ask for a sign?

5-12. Attuning our minds

I find this passage so thought-provoking. The Lord tells the disciples to beware of the leaven of the Pharisees and Sadducees; and these men who were so close to him, pre-occupied with earthly considerations, fail to understand.

Is that not typical of the way we listen to God, either in

reaction to our Bible reading or when listening to sermons, or even in prayer? Our personal concerns cloud our perception of what he is saying and we hear what relates to our current thinking and circumstances. The disciples already had their minds, guiltily, on bread; and the mention of yeast leapt out at them. It must have seemed that Christ had penetrated their thoughts. So they associated what he said with the subject on their minds instead of the subject on his mind.

Does this happen to us? Or more correctly, how often does it happen?

Yet in this passage there is no chance remark seized upon purely by coincidence. Jesus was aware of the disciples' association of his words with bread. They did not perceive the depth of what he said, but that does not mean the juxtaposition of their thoughts and his words was accidental. He was reaching out to their thoughts, but they were not sufficiently open to take the association and grasp its creative possibilities. I am sure that happens to all of us, all the time.

How often have I read a verse of Scripture one morning and twisted it to fit in with my problems? Sometimes we only look for comfort, when the Lord is giving us a challenge. We think we can take from the Bible what we want, instead of what God wants.

I am reminded of the Beatitude: blessed are the pure in heart, for they shall see God. I feel we are often, like the disciples, made opaque by our impurities. We cannot see with any clarity because our line of vision is cluttered with imperfections – even small ones like poor management of our domestic arrangements – which prevent us from receiving the light unhindered. We are burdened with problems and difficulties.

I heard a piercing sermon recently which emphasised that when Christ tells us to take up our cross and follow him, he is not talking about our day-to-day problems and difficulties, but the heroism of the Christian Way. Forgetting the shopping is not the essence of our spiritual life.

When the Lord speaks to us we must be listening with all our attention, having put the shopping aside.

Why do we find that so hard?

13-23. Taking God aside

Peter's profession of faith marks a turning point in the Gospel, as Jesus sets his face towards Jerusalem.

The Lord charges the disciples to tell no one that he is the Christ. We can look at that in several ways, but one of them is this: he says to them, I am sharing with you this world-shattering information. I am taking you into my confidence – God's confidence. You have the knowledge of the divine plan of salvation. You have my absolute trust.

What an amazing thing! That the eternal, almighty God of the universe can so treat his creatures! We should tremble in wonder at this verse.

And what comes next? A further, deeper revelation for the disciples. Christ begins to instruct them concerning his passion, death and resurrection. They are taken deeper into his confidence. He entrusts to them foreknowledge of both the horror and the glory. And their reaction is not to marvel but to be appalled.

Peter takes the Lord aside and begins to rebuke him. We can imagine the scene. Peter, perhaps the older man, a born leader whom the others can rely on as spokesman because he is inclined to speak his mind when the rest would show reserve – Peter puts what he believes is an older and wiser hand on a young shoulder and gives Christ a good talking-to. He does this in full awareness that he is speaking to the Messiah himself but he nevertheless feels he knows what's best.

The situation is not half as surprising as it sounds when we remember, honestly, the upstart nature of our own talk with God. This is what you should be doing, Lord. Here is my agenda for you to follow, my list of commands for you today. You seem to have forgotten what's going on in certain parts of the world and you're not handling so-and-so's life to their best advantage, so listen while I take you aside and point out where you're going wrong. I'm doing this for your own good because I care for your image. I can see what's best here on the ground, I have more experience of this life than you with your bare thirty years.

We have all done it, with the very best of intentions, and we often call it, piously, intercession. Peter 'took' Christ. Does that imply real physical contact, the literal hand on the shoulder, which so easily can lead to a twist of the arm?

What is Christ's reply? Imposing the human will on God is evil. There is a fine line, which we rarely discern, between asking in faith and arm-twisting. If our prayers are attuned to the will of God they will become vessels of the Kingdom; but if they are only attuned to our own desires they will distance us from the Lord.

The trouble is, we spend much of our time like a yo-yo going between the one situation and the other. Like Peter we can be so close to Christ that we see his glory, hear his most intimate revelations – and the next moment we become so blinded by this familiarity shown us by God that we fool ourselves into thinking it gives us the right to tell him what to do. How stupid! How can we make this mistake, how could Peter make this mistake? Yet we continue in our stupidity.

24-28. Taking on the Cross

I am writing these words on the feast of St Sergius of Radonezh, one of the most famous Russian monastic saints. Christ's command to take up our cross is at the heart of monasticism. Those who give their all know that what they lose in worldly terms is small in comparison with the glory they find in God.

We are often so bound up with earthly things that they crowd out our Christian life. But is there any other real life – outside the Kingdom? For instance, I am currently preparing to go on holiday. The packing and information-gathering going on in our household consume us with anticipation because what is to come is such a desired goal. Should we not be preparing in the same way – but ten-fold – for our arrival in heaven? Yet we generally act as if we are not on the journey there at all.

We are lulled into such dangerous complacence in our spiritual life! Meanwhile all the things which consume our lives are really consuming us and our relationship with God. We must be watchful that we do not miss Christ as he passes by and offers us our cross; and 'watch' is the very word he uses, that we enter not into the terrible temptation to indulge ourselves in that pernicious way which leads to inner death.

To deny ourselves is not to negate ourselves but to root out everything which mars the image of God in us, everything which puffs up our false ego at the expense of the divine will which longs to glorify us with the mind of Christ. If we lose all that binds us to the earth, to mortality, to sinfulness we will be crowned with eternity in that superabundance of life of which the Gospel speaks so beautifully. According to the measure we have participated in Christ's passion we will participate in his glory.

Part 5

ON THE WAY

Chapter 17

Darkness and light

1-13. The transfiguration

The last two verses of the preceding chapter have spoken of the Son of Man coming in the glory of his Father with his angels, and the promise that some of the disciples would not taste of death 'till they see the Son of Man coming in his Kingdom'.

And here we read of Jesus transfigured, shining with glory. Might not Peter, James and John have thought that moment promised by their Master had come? They see him radiant with divine light; they hear the voice of the Father echoing from the luminous cloud.

They are terrified by the experience of the Living God perceived in a way beyond that granted to other men. They fall on their faces in abject dismay. It is reminiscent of Isaiah and his vision in the Temple; and the shepherds at Bethlehem – incidents when, like this one, the fire of God comes so near that it threatens to consume.

There is a parallel here with Moses and Mount Sinai. When he comes down from the mountain after receiving the Law his face shone. It is no coincidence that in the monastery of St Catherine at the foot of Mount Sinai there is a mosaic of the Transfiguration. Moses prefigures Christ, and shines with reflected glory. Christ shines with his own divine light.

Even his garments shone. His divinity pervaded not only the physical matter of his body but even the matter of ordinary woven cloth. The everyday stuff of this world became capable of being filled with God, a sign of that day when 'God shall be all in all'. What inspiration this is for our concern for all creation, our care for the environment! What hope this gives our human clay! We can all become the burning bush of Sinai, permeated by God but not consumed – instead fulfilled, transfigured into glorious vessels of the divine will. And this can happen now, as we draw ever nearer to Christ in the Gospels and learn to put his words into action. We have the power, like his disciples, to transfigure our whole lives.

But I am speaking with hindsight. The disciples on Mount Tabor can only look, and tremble in utter confusion. Whatever bells this happening may have rung in their consciousness – and those verses of Chapter 16 were also concerned with judgement – they are at a complete loss how to behave. Peter blurts out words in disconcertion. The confident adviser who had taken his young Master aside and rebuked him only a week previously now falls at his feet in adoration and fear.

What comes over to me is the disciples' sudden awareness not only of God's majesty but of their own utter unworthiness. They have no right to be in this awesome place, witnessing almost unspeakable things.

Is this how we will feel when we meet Christ in eternity? I believe it is. But it is not what we commonly imagine. We want to see the familiar, human face of Jesus, the one we have pictured healing the sick and scooping up children in his loving arms – not the sight of divinity too bright to bear, the terrifying light of his glory.

How do I come into his presence day by day? Is it not with something of the back-slapping pallyness which often passes, in our modern society, for affection? Is it not in the spirit of the television chat show, immediate Christian name terms and casual manners? Where is my sense of awe at being in the presence of the Living God, the creator of the universe, my saviour and judge?

We can only be scooped up in Jesus' arms if we have the innocence – innocence from sin and evil – of little children. We can only address God as Father if we so possess the mind of Christ, the will of Christ, that we can in him participate, however incipiently, in sonship.

The light of the Transfiguration shows up the murky places within us where we have never allowed God to penetrate. Certainly transfiguration is possible; we can open the dungeons of our souls to Christ, he is waiting breathless for us to do so. But we must be prepared for the experience to be humbling, overwhelming, unimaginably terrifying.

O Lord, penetrate our dark side, the inner reaches of our godlessness, and change us into vessels of light!

14-21. Down to earth

Peter, James and John have had a shattering experience. They have seen the veil of Jesus' humanity lifted for an instant to reveal his divinity. They have 'beheld his glory' as St Peter says in his second Epistle (2 Pet 1:16). They have heard the Father's voice.

And now they are on their way back down to earth. How must they have felt, walking beside this man whom they had seen transfigured beyond humanity? Were they stunned into silent reverence, following his footsteps with new determination to direct their lives after his? Were they bursting with questions, perhaps holding back in embarrassment for him to start the conversation? Were they longing to tell the other disciples what had happened?

Christ speaks. 'Tell no one the vision, until the Son of Man is raised from the dead.' This precipitates their questions – if they do not ask now, there will be no opportunity once they are back among the others, in whose presence they must keep silence.

So this time is given them to speak, and the Lord answers them. And they understand what he means.

There is a time given to all of us to ask questions; a time to keep silent about what has been revealed; a time, the Lord's time, to speak out. When we ask at the right time he gives us understanding.

That can happen to us when we read the Gospel. One day a certain passage will be obscure, another day it will speak clearly. Our first task is to store them up. The temptation, when a verse does not 'speak', is to shut one's mind to it at every subsequent reading also. We skim over familiar words in our eagerness to reach the next passage compatible with our own thoughts. The Lord gives us to understand if we are willing to let him open the conversation, and then be ready to put our questions and grasp the reply.

What happens when the disciples reach the others? A crowd has formed, waiting for the Master because his followers are trying their hand at healing and not being successful.

And Christ accuses them – disciples, crowd, the whole generation – of faithlessness. The account in St Mark elaborates. The father of the epileptic boy cries out, 'Lord, I believe. Help my unbelief!' – the cry of every one of us at some time or another.

Now, is 'faithless' the opposite of 'faithful' or 'full of faith'? Certainly we need straightforward belief; but the Gospel will go on to say in verse 21 that this kind of healing can only be accomplished by faith in action – faithfulness – by prayer and fasting.

What is Christ's response to this faithlessness? Does he turn aside in disgust? No. He has taken on himself to show faithfulness, fulfiled in prayer and fasting, on our behalf. He heals the boy. Both the father's requests are answered.

22-27. Sharing the darkness

For the second time Jesus foretells his death and resurrection. The first warning provoked an outburst of rebellion by Peter. This time no one dares speak a word of opposition. Perhaps they now understand Christ's resolution. Nevertheless they are 'greatly distressed'.

Do we ever expect to be distressed by our faith? Do we

accept that there will be times when Christ will tell us painful things we would rather not hear? I think we fool ourselves if we persist in thinking that the time after the Resurrection and Pentecost is all light. No; we too must share with our Lord the darkness and distress which the evil of the world brings to the human condition.

But we must remember that this darkness is never separated from the brightness of the Easter dawn. In one breath Christ speaks of death and resurrection. We must always do the same.

Chapter 18

Dealing with sin

1-11. Dealing with temptation

This passage goes into some detail about being a temptation. We should be very careful about how we treat children, the Lord tells us. It is so easy to cause them to lose their innocence and to grow up into the sinful ways of the world. So, he says, we should be absolutely ruthless about anything in us which causes ourselves or others to be tempted.

His language is vivid. Cut off your hand or your foot; beware of being thrown into the eternal fires of hell. Strong stuff, this.

And these words are spoken in front of a child, whom he has called forward and placed in front of the disciples. Be like this child, he says, be humble and innocent and vulnerable – not abject drudges but free, happy and with an innocent sense of wonder. Retain those precious childlike qualities which adults are usually all too keen to shed in their eagerness to be seen as men of the world, sophisticated and mature. If you wish to grow, to reach the full stature of the Christian vision, return first to the infancy of your humanity, the purity of your state in Eden before the Fall.

Only, like this child, you must do it surrounded by a difficult and hostile world. Just as this boy is dwarfed by the ring of adults around him, just as he is exposed to harsh words and the talk of hell fire, so you will have to live in this adulterous and sinful generation.

12-20. *Dealing with sinners*

The parable of the lost sheep is here set in a different context from that of St Luke's Gospel, where Jesus tells it in answer to the Pharisees' carping that he mixes with sinners.

In Matthew he likens the lost sheep not to tax collectors but to innocent little children. Perhaps that should remind us that we must not limit a parable's relevance to too narrow a context; Jesus must have repeated his parables and teaching many times over in a variety of circumstances during his ministry.

As far as this parable is concerned, it can show us that God's infinite, searching care is for all of us, whether we are lost because of our own wilful sins or because of the mishandling of our elders and betters. In the Lord's eyes we all remain children, just as much in need of protection as vulnerable sheep, and the objects of his loving will that all should be saved.

How, then do these words hang together with the next verses, which speak of putting out of the Church community sinners who are unrepentant? How do we hold in balance God's desire for our salvation and the exiling of sinners?

Well, it is easy if we place ourselves self-righteously in the 'saved' camp and delight in the damnation of our neighbour; but I am not looking at the question from that viewpoint.

I see this as the inevitable matter of the rooting out of evil. None of us can conceive of evil existing in God's Kingdom; so if the Church is truly to be the Kingdom present on earth she must prune herself ruthlessly, just as we as individuals must subject ourselves to constant pruning. That does not preclude our constant vocation to seek out the lost. But both lost and found sheep must keep themselves in a continuous state of repentance in order to remain within God's realm of love, and at a distance from the destructive forces of evil.

There is another aspect to being in God's realm of love. It involves being of one mind – the mind of Christ. This communion of mind in love is a Kingdom prerequisite, which my own Church acknowledges with the words immediately preceding the Creed in our Liturgy: 'Let us love one another, that with one mind we may acknowledge Father, Son and Holy Spirit, consubstantial, life-giving Trinity'. Without this one mind in love we can neither pledge ourselves to God in the Creed nor come to Christ in Communion.

In this situation which should exist in the Church, it follows naturally that God's power to bind and to loose will be manifest, for it will be Christ who speaks, and Christ who prays, indwelling his Body of believers in mind and heart and will. So by the physical presence of the sacramental priesthood he can offer us forgiveness, or if necessary keep us outside the realms of the Kingdom until the evil in us has been eradicated.

But whether we are inside or out we still remain sheep, ultimately in the care of the one Shepherd who will never tire of searching for us every time we go astray.

21-35. Restoring relationships

We all know that as Christians we ought to forgive, but very often we do not know how. Yet until we learn to do so our own place in the Kingdom, our relationship with Christ which we treasure above everything else, can never be right.

How often do we wish that certain people could go away, could be forgotten, could cease to exist for us. We do not want them to be part of our life. Would we not also prefer certain people not to be in eternity with us? How could we endure to stand in God's presence forever beside so-and-so? And we may be equally unwilling to share the Lord's Table with them.

Sometimes, though one would like to heal that sorry

136

situation – to restore as well as to forgive. Again one does not always know how. Lord, when someone has offended or hurt me, or shattered my trust in them, how can that pain be healed? How can I return with them to the relationship which was ours before, especially if the other person refuses reconciliation? Wanting is not always enough. There has to be a practical way of going about putting things right. Sometimes, even after considerable prayer, one is not able to discern how to go about it.

Christ's command is to forgive not just with the intellect but 'from your heart'. The roots of evil weeds have to be dug out completely, or else they will sprout as soon as they are watered with fresh offence.

Well, that is the nature with weeds, and Peter obviously had experience of it. His brother had offended him over and over. Surely he was justified in reaching breaking point?

No, says Christ. Do you really want there to be a limit to forgiveness? Do you really want God in turn to say 'enough is enough'? Restoration of the human relationship with God is the very thing Jesus came to bring. We as 'little Christs' can therefore hardly do anything less. If we put a limit to our forgiveness we have fallen away from this restored relationship, we have put ourselves outside the very Kingdom we proclaim.

Chapter 19

The cost of faithfulness

1-12. Divorce

Adultery, the breaking of a relationship – one of the three
sins giving rise in the Early Church to automatic excom-
munication (the others being murder and apostasy) – pre-
supposes like them a spiritual breakdown. In the Orthodox
Church, which permits divorce for the cause of adultery, a
divorced person should therefore receive a period of spiritual re-training before being allowed to remarry.

It would be nice to think that the hardness of heart
recognised by Moses was not found among Christians.
Alas! We all know that is not the case. Like the disciples
we are sometimes tempted to think of marriage in terms of
expediency instead of sacrificial love.

Married people, like would-be celibates, are not all capable of receiving the strictest ideals. We can struggle
towards them, but when we go astray we know God's
mercy is bigger than our sorry attempts at rule-keeping.

13-26. Counting the cost

The picture of Jesus laying hands on the children is
surely the world's favourite. Cynics and sophisticates may
turn aside from it as a sign that they have grown out of such
simple sentiments but that only proves the point of the
episode for the rest of us. That trusting, simple, direct
response of open-hearted love is the essence of a true
relationship with God.

By contrast, the rich young man had lost that power to respond. He comes face to face with Christ, is stung by the look of love in his eyes, as Mark tells us, but cannot respond because of his enslavement to his possessions. He can only turn away in pain, aware that wealth has robbed him of something incalculable.

There is a terrible message in that, which Jesus spells out to his disciples. Being rich in worldly terms does not bring freedom and choice but the opposite. It cements us to the earth, it cements us within an ever-decreasing frame of mind; it cements our hearts so that they become stone.

That is all, tragically, fact; not so much God's judgement on the rich but the description of an inevitable process. Yet we in the Western world take it as the harmless norm. Very few of us would dream of giving up our comfortable lifestyle in order to follow Christ, not because we have consciously preferred our riches to him but because we do not see the choice as necessary. It doesn't apply to us, not these days, not in this country. Christ does not ask this question any more. He merely points us to the get-out clause: 'with God all things are possible'. There is no point in striving to do the impossible if he is all set to do it for us.

I am very wary of our tendency to adjust the Gospel in that way. Of course I recognise God's ultimate power to free us from any form of enslavement. But why do we so determinedly prefer that enslavement to the freedom he offers?

How many of us, when fighting moments of depression or doubt, would give anything for the chance to look into Christ's face, see him incontrovertibly before our eyes? And, were that given us, how many would then snatch back that anything as too costly, and turn away?

27-30. *Accepting Christ's freedom*

Eschatology, the study of the age to come, is a woolly business. Christ tells us so little about heaven that things can hardly be otherwise. What he concentrates on is giving us the Kingdom now, so that as we learn to live more and more in God's presence, making his laws – indeed his very life – our own, we grow into a union which, we will come to know from experience, can never be broken, only deepened.

But in this passage Jesus is more specific. The disciples are promised thrones, and the rest of us 'a hundredfold'.

A hundredfold of what? Of everything we have first given up for him; possessions, family, earthly inheritance.

The disciples, we are reminded by Peter himself, have given up everything for Christ; literally. He has become their whole life, and that relationship will continue for eternity.

What about us? Here I am writing these lines in a comfortable house, surrounded by family, the latest electrical goods, money in the bank... I cannot in honesty say that I have given up any of these things for Christ.

Very few of us can. I do have a Christian friend who has lived most of her life with no more possessions than she can fit into a cupboard; and she has also lost most of her family. Where is her 'hundredfold'? In human terms she has not been rewarded at all. Her life remains hard and she cuts a rather unhappy figure; her sacrifices do not even encourage others to follow her example. I don't know how the Church bigwigs and the 'Success Gospel' afficionados will feel when they see her called 'up higher' in eternity. Christ has an affinity with the despised – as he himself was despised – and most of us have an affinity, alas, with the despisers.

'Many that are first will be last, and the last first.' Under Christ's strict, literal criteria we can only place ourselves among those destined to be brought down a few pegs. The comfortable answer is to move the goal posts in our direction and say this is not meant to be taken literally, not in our day when Christianity is the established religion and it would be plainly impracticable for us all to sell the house and car and take to the streets. We make the odd psycho-

140

logical sacrifice, we support worthy charities and give up our spare time for Christian concerns. It is true to say that most of us are trapped by circumstances into that sort of lifestyle.

I think a lot depends on the way we are trapped. Do I look at my God-given situation and promise the Lord to bring his will to it? Do I use my possessions primarily for his glory and his work, bringing the light of Christ into the ungodly reaches of mammon as far as I can? Do I move in my day-to-day life as one who is free, who can use it as a tool in God's service, or am I the tool, enslaved by things, by people, by the world's standards? Am I really trapped, or has Christ given me the power of inner freedom from everything around me?

His service is perfect freedom. 'Be free!' he says to us in this passage. 'Refuse to be enslaved by the clutter and cares of modern living. Be free to be filled with the Spirit and to be blown where he wills. If that will calls you to leave worldliness behind in a literal way, follow joyfully. If it calls you to stay in its midst but untouched by its corruption, free from its stranglehold, accept that also with joy.'

In either case what we should hand over to God is our all, in every sense that he seeks it, and leave it to him to give back what is good for us.

Lord, all things are possible with you. Grant me the courage to accept the freedom you offer, and to see worldly enslavement for what it is.

Chapter 20

Servant and master

1-16. God's generosity

Here we see God's freedom in action – his freedom to shower his blessings on whoever he chooses, not because we deserve them or demand them but simply because he loves us.

This does, of course run contrary to all our notions of justice, and the common juridical view of the Last Judgement as being set out like a familiar human court of law. Instead it is about calling us into a relationship; into relationship with God, into citizenship of his Kingdom.

I am reminded of what the word 'kingdom' meant to people in New Testament times, before the advent of constitutional monarchies: a realm where the monarch had absolute power. The king not only ruled, but owned the land and sometimes the people. His every whim was law.

Now, we know – Christ demonstrated – that our King, our Master, is the slave who girds himself with a towel and washes our feet. Yet his rule is still absolute. Christ does not talk about the democracy of heaven. God's Kingship is all good and does not take into consideration our evil ways, which may masquerade as fairness but in reality are based on self-promotion and greed.

We can see those very characteristics at work in the parable. The labourers hired early in the day struck a fair bargain, but in the light of the eleventh-hour workers receiving the same they suddenly wanted extra. Maintaining pay differentials, it's called today; another name for not loving one's neighbour as oneself but instead furthering one's own cause. After all, it was not the eleventh-hour workers who asked that their longer-toiling brethren should receive more!

Taking all this out of the labour market and into a spiritual context, we can see that this is how we often react to salvation and our relationship with God. Will the death-bed convert, after a life of riotous living and atheism, really find himself next to me in heaven, or even more preposter-ously, having just scraped in at the lowest place be exalted to the top table while I languish at the far end? Will adher-ents of that despised and heretical sect be as welcome as my co-religionists? Will all our frantic churchy doings count for nothing while the half-hearted, passive pew-fod-der we see around us walk brazenly through the pearly gates at our side? We don't like to consider such possibili-ties. We are the prodigal son's elder brother, full of right-eous – we think – indignation, not to say a fair measure of jealousy. We don't like to see God acting gratuitously. We want him to conform to our self-enhancing rules. The alter-native is, in our opinion, monstrous. We can only allow him to love the loveless on our conditions, which maintain a tidy pecking order.

Yes, we do begrudge God his generosity, as one transla-tion renders verse 15. We need to remember continually the promise of verse 16: 'so the last will be first, and the first last.' Despite all our so-called Christian living, despite our Church activities and holier than thou stance, we must always count ourselves unprofitable servants.

And we must take to heart that word 'unprofitable'. We are never worthless. In God's eyes we are all worth dying for – and that is not just in theory; he has died for us. But our worth is in our being, not our doing. What we do is as nothing, but we must be like Christ, humble and totally selfless. Then we will discover, with joy, that God's gratui-tous love is directed at us, because in the realm of divine justice it is we who are the eleventh-hour labourers.

Christ promises the disciples that they will have thrones of honour in the Kingdom, and judge the twelve tribes of Israel. And he tells the vineyard parables.

How much time elapsed between all this and the beginning of the episode we cannot tell. Was the picture of the thrones still fresh in the disciples' minds? That is not a promise you forget easily. No doubt it coloured their interpretation of the vineyard parable; surely that must apply to the Pharisees rather than to them?

Then the Lord speaks to them of his coming passion and death – not just in vague terms but in the starkest possible; he will be crucified. And he will be raised on the third day.

This time Peter does not protest. The talk of the Kingdom has blunted the sharpness of torture and death since they first heard Christ speak of it. What they focus on now is not the Lord's suffering but their share in his victory.

Peter had already been promised the keys of the Kingdom at Caesarea Philippi. What will be the reward for the other two in the inner triumvirate, James and John? They come with their mother and she asks a favour. Where Peter with his keys might sit is not her concern. May her sons have the choice thrones, on either side of Christ?

This is a very human passage. We are tempted to see the archetypal Jewish mother, anxious to push her boys forward. 'To you be the passion, to my sons be the glory already.'

Christ replies with a challenge. Can they drink the bitter cup that will be his? Mark's Gospel adds 'or be baptized with the baptism with which I am baptized?' The brothers say they can.

This is not just a challenge to them but to each one of us. It is the question which my bishop deliberately asks every man who seeks ordination. It is, he says, not a warning but a promise. Should it not apply to us all? If you follow me this will happen, says Christ. Persecution is what the Christian should expect as the norm. Even if it does not happen literally, one has no right to be a follower of Christ without being prepared to follow him to Calvary.

And what comes after is not a right at all. Christ himself does not grant the places of honour; how dare we take them for ourselves? If we see ourselves as nothing more than unprofitable slaves who have only done our allotted task we will truly be following in the footsteps of our Master who himself came to serve.

The disciples had, in that sinister way we all do, seized on the talk of the Kingdom and translated it into terms of worldly power, instead of seeing it according to the divine perspective of self-offering in love. The Kingdom – and that should mean also the Church, and the life of every Christian – is not organised according to human power structures and patterns of domination. If we want to be part of the Kingdom we must kneel at the feet of Christ and every person made in his image.

29-34. *Transforming prayer*

The cry of these two blind men, 'Have mercy on us, Son of David!' is very close to our Orthodox Jesus Prayer. It is the cry from the heart, the cry of desperation, and therefore utter dependence. All the blind men's hope is in it. If they do not shout their loudest, *now*, as Jesus passes, it will be for ever too late; he will never pass this way again. All their will is in this cry, all their life, all their faith; all their deepest selves.

That bears no relation to our everyday polite prayer to the Lord. I know there are times when I pray out of the depths, when my whole self is collected in a shout of pain or despair – or gratitude. On those occasions I probably suffer from the same fault as these men: my primary concern is really my own needs and circumstances, not God. Nevertheless I can at least say that my prayer at such times is true; not a recitation to which I give only half my attention but words wrung from my soul. There are other days when all I can say to God is that I am in too much pain to talk to him at all, and ask him to accept my silence.

All this is nothing like what is sometimes dangerously made of the Jesus Prayer: a kind of Christian mantra in which not even the mind, let alone the heart, is involved. No. We must begin again and learn to put our whole selves into this cry, for only then shall we see the Lord.

Perhaps the most interesting feature of this incident is the reaction of the blind men when they are healed. They follow Christ. They do not get up and go home – perhaps they had no home? – or turn their backs on him as soon as they have what they want. They continue in that hope and trust which they had given him.

They were not only given sight, but the privilege of seeing God Incarnate before their eyes. They were given insight: the sure knowledge that they had come face to face with the Messiah, the Son of David. First that had been, in their cry, a matter of faith. Now it was certainty, of which they were living proof. They had received a vision of the Kingdom, and they went on to live by it.

Is that my experience? When my desperate cry of prayer is answered, does it lead me to the Kingdom or back to my own preoccupations? Our prayers – all our prayers – must make a real difference to our lives. They must have cataclysmic results. They must transform us beyond recognition, change our lives irrevocably and completely. That is real answered prayer – when we answer God.

Part 6

JERUSALEM

Chapter 21

Teaching in the Temple

1-17. Challenging the Temple

The sight of Jerusalem from the Mount of Olives is still impressive today but when the Temple of God dominated the landscape it must have brought tears to the eyes of every Jew. And here we see God himself come to take possession of his Temple.

Those with open hearts rejoice; but the hierarchy to whom the Temple had been entrusted take offence at Jesus; he threatens their religious authority, their material prosperity, their power and status. He challenges their self-righteous autonomy.

Doesn't he do exactly the same with us? He challenges all our priorities – financial concerns, independence, sense of power – and if we are listening, very often he says a stark 'No!' But generally we are like the money-changers. We are so preoccupied with our own business that we simply do not hear his voice above all the hubbub. When he steps in and overturns the tables of those false priorities we are indignant.

No doubt they were initially pleased at Christ's presence. It was good for business! Is that how we see him, as advantageous to our worldly comfort?

And what happens when that advantage suddenly becomes a threat, when Christ oversteps the very limited authority I give him in my life? As soon as I sense my own eclipse I start raising objections, just like the chief priests and scribes. Should I not be the master of my own house?

But Christ calls the Temple his house. Am I not also his temple – the temple of the Holy Spirit, a veritable house of prayer? Should not my thoughts and conversation be a continual 'hosanna', not a market-place of gossip and thieving desires? Am I a source of perfect praise or ungodly indignation?

If the latter, am I conscious of the Lord leaving me and going to lodge somewhere more amenable? Yes, he will return another day; but how can I make him more welcome, more truly at home in this living temple of my heart?

Lord, I need to overturn so many worldly things in my life which hinder your presence. I need to remove the dross, the material accretions, the sources of unholy contamination; I need to take drastic action. I know you are prepared to help me drive out every trace of evil. I realise this will be an unpleasant, perhaps painful process but without it there will be no room for you to come and heal, no place for me to sing your praises. Lord, cast me not away from your face and take not your Holy Spirit from the temple of my soul and body!

18-22. Answering prayer

Christ calls us to a faith which is difficult, when we consider the fig tree, but one which ultimately works if we are prepared to surrender all our concerns to him.

Nevertheless that is all too often not what we make of faith. His words about moving mountains are taken by some as the rationale for the Santa Claus approach to God, where prayer is reduced to a list of requests. What are people who think like that going to say when they come face to face with the Lord in eternity, when there is nothing left for which to ask?

Of course there are occasions when we ask God specific things. I know from experience that he answers these prayers when it is right to do so; and one must leave what is right to his judgement. However, there is a difference between a self-centred shopping list and intercession born of love for others.

When we pray for, say, famine victims our prayer should imply, 'show me, Lord, how I can fulfil your will to feed the starving.' Ultimately all our prayer involves the joining of our will to God's. If we so trust God, so believe in his love and mercy because our hearts, minds and wills are at one with him, then whatever we ask in prayer will be according to his purpose. We will have created the conditions of the Kingdom, in which God is free to act – through us.

23-32. A stern reply

Discernment is a spiritual gift often ignored nowadays, but here we see Jesus himself glowing with it. He sees straight to the heart of his questioners and understands their reply as the excuse that it is.

How often do we come to him with an excuse – and are surprised when he refuses in his infinite wisdom to be drawn by it?

It is interesting to note the motives of the chief priests and elders. They are not on the side of God, nor of public opinion; they care about nothing but their own reputation. Against such an attitude the Lord will have no dialogue. Instead he quietly exerts his ultimate authority, beyond which it is not possible for humanity to penetrate: 'Neither will I tell you.'

Perhaps when we receive that answer from him the first thing we should ponder is whether our asking has overstepped the legitimate bounds of the Kingdom situation of the previous verses.

But how easy it is for us to think we inhabit the Kingdom by right! Like the religious establishment of Jesus' day and the first son of the parable we say all the right words – automatically in our rote prayers every day. What we need is not response of the lips but of the heart, Christ tells us: we must let our pious words penetrate our hearts, so that we truly see, believe and repent.

33-46. The folly of love

This parable begins so ingenuously; the picture Jesus paints is such a pleasant pastoral scene.

And at first it continues in the same vein. The owner, still ingenuous, sends his servants on routine business – and suddenly it all turns sour. Instead of repaying his trust the tenants seize the opportunity to rebel.

This ingenuousness of God: is it not the folly of love? We see it still in verse 37. He is willing to trust his fickle creatures to the utmost because he loves them even to death.

The terrifying thing about the tenants' response is their awareness. They know exactly who the son is and they make their evil plans accordingly. This is brought home to us all the way through the Gospel. Christ's enemies did not seek to destroy him because they were unaware of his Messiahship but precisely because they were aware of it. There was no case of mistaken identity. They never doubted his miracles, they never denied his powers. They saw, they hated, they consciously sought to kill not a false Messiah but the true one. Here was their chance to murder God himself and become free; and they took it.

As we shall see in a matter of a few pages, that horrifying scenario was a prophecy about to be fulfiled. The chief priests and Pharisees of verse 45 really did have Christ taken and killed.

For us, of course, it does not end there. We sit smugly waiting for the owner to come and hand the vineyard to us Christians who – naturally – would not dream of doing anything other than giving him its fruits multiplied a hundredfold.

Oh yes? Was not the cry 'God is dead' of a few years

back shouted not in anguish but in triumph – and by Christian theologians? Do we not murder Christ anew every time we act knowingly against his will?

So will the Kingdom be taken away from us? Perhaps; but the owner, we know, will be waiting with the robe we left behind, ready to embrace us when we come to our senses and return. The folly of the ingenuous love of the Cross cannot be quenched by our pathetic human hatreds, just as the immortal God cannot die without rising.

Chapter 22

A new vision of the Kingdom

1-14. The banquet of the Kingdom

The King's wedding feast differs from the other Kingdom parables in that it describes more than how the
Kingdom grows or how it attracts people; it describes
the Kingdom of heaven itself. True, Christ paints no de-
tailed picture of the banquet, beyond saying it is ready,
the table is groaning, and that it is the wedding-feast of
the King's Son. But that is enough for us to visualise a
sumptuous meal, a celebration unrivalled in its bountiful
and happy nature; and the focus of the proceedings, the
proud Father delighting in the Son and his bride. It is a
never-ending extravaganza of joy bearing not the least
resemblance to clouds, harps and eternal boredom which
is the commonplace picture of heaven!

It reminds me inevitably of Easter, of our Orthodox
midnight service which is four hours of colour and noise
and overflowing exuberance. That is no accident – the
resurrection celebration *is* participation in the Kingdom
here and now. And so, too is every Liturgy, every Communion service. Our deliberately joyful and beautiful worship is designed to be 'heaven on earth' in a very real sense.
So we can say from experience that we understand Christ's
description of the Kingdom because we have entered into
its beauty, however briefly, ourselves.

But the celebration of a wedding is more than this. It is
primarily a matter of relationships – between two people
becoming organically one. This is the perfect picture of
Christ and his bride, the Church. We are not just to be

154

guests at this marriage. We are to be the bride.

And the 'we' is important. It is not as individuals that we are betrothed to the Lord but as members of one body. Indeed we, this body the Church, become through the marriage members of his Body; one flesh with him.

This is exactly what Communion is. To reduce it to a memorial or a symbol is not what the Kingdom is about. Communion *is* the Kingdom, not an earthly mock-up but the real thing, exactly as the Lord promised that the Kingdom is within us first of all.

What can we think of the people who refused to come to the King's Banquet, and of the man who entered without his wedding garment? Well, we know that the majority turns its back on the Church. The Kingdom is realised week by week and the uninterested make their excuses. And the man with no wedding garment?

According to Jewish custom the wedding garments were handed out to the guests on their arrival. Here was an individual who had somehow refused it. There is pride here. Is it the pride of self-importance, the pride of heresy or the pride of unrepentance? Is it the pride of one who has not refused to come, but will only come on his own terms?

The wedding garment is the garment of humility. I am reminded of one of our Holy Week hymns: 'I see the bridal chamber adorned, O my Saviour, but I have no wedding garment to enter there. Make the robe of my soul to shine, O giver of light, and save me.'

Does that not sum up all that is wrong with us? Is this worthless pride what we would cling to rather than accept the Lord's bounty?

15-22. *The image of God*

I remember as a child of ten hearing this passage and being impressed by the wisdom of Jesus' reply.

His adversaries attack him with a two-edged sword; he will fall foul of either the Romans or the Jewish nationalists. He transforms it into a two-sided coin; if they accept Roman prosperity they must be prepared to give the system its due.

But the coin – a literal coin – reveals a deeper message. The image on it is Caesar's, not only a bitter reminder of foreign domination but in terms of the Mosaic Law a transgression of the commandment on idolatry. You can either serve the image of material gain or the Living God who has no image.

Yet God does have an image: each one of us is made in the divine image. As the coin belongs to Caesar, so we belong to God. We should render our whole selves to him. We can give our worldly possessions back whence they came but God demands not a few coins now and then, not a tithe of what we own or the modicum of time we are prepared to allocate to the 'religious' bit of our lives, but what is his, our totality. There is nothing of us which is not stamped with his image, which does not belong to him unreservedly.

That is very easy to forget. Like coins we get our share of rough handling and the image becomes worn down, covered in grime, all but obliterated with life's harsh treatment so that it is no longer plain for us or for others to recognise. But it is never lost completely; it is always there at the core of each person, waiting to be restored by God who made us in the beginning. We never lose our intrinsic value.

And if we pine over our imperfect image we can look up from our self-absorption into the face of Jesus the perfect Image of God.

The Pharisees could literally have done that. They were amazed by his words. So what was their response? Did they look into his face and see there the perfect Image challenging the latent image within themselves? Or did they keep their eyes fixed on the coin, eager to snatch it back from Christ and make off with it as quickly as possible?

What about us? When we open the Bible do we see Jesus as the perfect image of what we could be? Do we see him in our neighbour, whether in the holiness of someone who is close to him or in the need of the distressed? Did I see anything of the divine image in myself the last time I looked in a mirror?

If not, why not? This is a pressing question, because if we keep the Lord's image buried within ourselves, how will other people ever come to see him?

23-45. *Words of truth*

'He is not God of the dead but of the living' speaks to the bereaved, the dying, the agonised doubters. These are not the veiled words of a parable, the 'work it out for yourself' answer Christ sometimes gave but straight talking, the definitive word which he reserves for occasions when he wants to leave no doubt about his meaning. Like his command to the woman taken in adultery, 'Go and sin no more', and the various times he said 'Follow me', this is a decisive statement which we must accept or reject without any speculative meandering.

These decisive statements share the quality of being either a joy or a terror. To the rich young ruler, 'follow me' spoke of a price he was not prepared to pay; he was forced to turn his back on Christ because his words spelt the end of everything he held to be dear. The disciples on the other hand heard the same words as the message of salvation and could not fail to respond.

Jesus tells the Sadducees plainly, 'You are wrong.' Have we ever heard him say that to us? Have we ever considered we may have misinterpreted his words, in Scripture or in prayer? We may often admit to coming to a fuller understanding but rarely that we need to recast our understanding completely.

This is worrying. Have I really so attuned myself to the mind of Christ that I understand everything he says? Is not his word far beyond anything my finite human intelligence can comprehend?

And, he tells us, the truth beyond our understanding is so much more beautiful than anything we can in our arrogance imagine.

There comes a point when we should, like the Pharisees and Sadducees, see the futility of continually probing and testing God. We should simply be able to stand back, not with the fear of his adversaries who retired to their corner smarting with wounded pride but with the holy fear of having touched the hem of his garment. We should prostrate in awe and wonder, and truly, like David, acknowledge him as our Lord.

Chapter 23

The wrong way

1-12. *Practising what we preach*

Not practising what one preaches must be the most common criticism levelled against Christians. It puts us back on a par with the Pharisees, something we do not relish.

We feel there is a difference. We fail through weakness, not deliberate pride. We may be second-rate but at least we are aware of that, we don't suffer from the Pharisees' false arrogance. We don't parade our religious zeal.

Or perhaps our piety is just more subtle. We don't wear distinctive clothes but we do sometimes wear our churchy activities a touch more brazenly than we should. I have heard people admire me for enduring a particularly long journey to church each week – over fifty miles – and I can almost hear their silent thoughts: 'and what good has it done her? She's no better than the rest of us.'

How often do I use my church membership as a status symbol, a tool for deriding the unchurched? I may in pious moments be willing to think of myself as a servant of God but not of my neighbours, even Christian ones. I try to justify that by looking for an interpretation of verses 11 and 12 which salves my conscience.

After all, think what would happen if our Church prelates took these words seriously and started cleaning the floors and acting as servers to their subordinates!

Well, such things do – rarely – happen. We only need the light of one exception to show up the murky behaviour of the rest of us.

We can see the perfect example in Jesus himself. But

how did the Pharisees around him react? How would our contemporaries react against us if we followed the Lord's example literally? Would we too not end up the victim of humiliation, outcast and crucified?

I'm afraid we would. That is, after all, what Christ promises us; the exaltation of the humble is not for this life. No wonder, then that we actively prefer not to practise what we preach, since the Gospel preached properly is so uncomfortable in worldly terms!

13-39. *The Pharisee in us*

The 'woes' Jesus addresses to the Pharisees are also directed at us. We are just as guilty of hedging our faults with pious terms and concocting our own rules to justify them, making us suitably religious-looking on the outside but as putrescent as corpses within. I know myself how I can spout all the theory of my faith but I do not live it. There is no inner change. What am I to do about this?

I find these Gospel words particularly vivid since my own recent visit to Jerusalem. I have seen the tombs in the Kidron Valley. I had Christ's prayer for Jerusalem ringing in my ears as I stood on the Mount of Olives. His maternal concern for the city, his heartfelt cry of loving sadness at the fate of the community which rejected him, his acceptance of it without any of the desire to dominate as is so often the case with us – all this is also directed at us if we take on the mantle of the Pharisees!

It is so easy to see in these words of Christ a prophecy fulfiled and therefore no longer generally applicable. Yes, the Pharisees did get their come-uppance, but so will we if we do not take the Lord seriously. We must struggle to keep our hearts capable of being wounded by these words, so that they may cauterize in this life, not consume us in the next.

Chapter 24

The last days

1-12. Love grows cold

There are some terrifying pictures painted in this passage. The first is of the destruction of the Temple – a marvel of architecture, solid and massive, and yet as Christ foretold soon to be completely razed to the ground.

Then we have wars and natural disasters, continuing sources of horror never far away from human experience.

Then persecution of the Church. That, we like to think, is behind us; but in fact the twentieth century has seen persecution far greater than anything devised by Imperial Rome.

The most chilling terror of all is surely the prophecy of verse 12: that human love will grow cold.

As Christians we are supposed to love our neighbour as ourselves. Most of us do not reach that perfection but at least we strive towards it. In the world at large human love is found mostly within the family situation.

Yet increasingly in our society family life is breaking down. Men and women treat each other purely as objects of exploitation, children are dragged up in violent, loveless conditions. The false prophets of the culture of greed hammer home their selfish message daily. Human love truly seems to be growing cold.

I don't think we should judge this smugly as a sign of the end; it is not for us to know the times, Christ tells us. But I do believe it is our duty as Christians to stand out as family people, establishing our little outposts of the Kingdom in which love rules supreme. '*Most* men's love will grow cold', the Lord says; it is up to us to keep firmly among the faithful minority.

13-28. *Enduring the end*

This passage begins with those striking words of encouragement: 'But he who endures to the end will be saved.' They must have kept so many Christians going when they faced torture or long spells of imprisonment under persecution. I am thinking of members of my own congregation; and John Bunyan, who suffered here in Bedford from where I write. One can also include all those who face the agonies of incurable and excruciating illness.

But what do most of us have to endure? Not so much that is horrendous, but quite a lot of wearing triviality and boredom. Day to day life muddles on and we are caught up with the minutiae of secular culture in which our faith does not seem to have a great role to play. Cleaning the house, keeping the garden under, the weekly trip to the supermarket, a routine job – all these can be mindless. Furthermore they can weigh us down, wear us down into thinking this is all that life has to offer. Our Christianity can easily begin to ebb away beneath a burden of nothingness.

In theory these are such small things to 'endure to the end' but in practice Satan uses them very effectively. It is heartening to remember how tedious life must have been as a provincial carpenter/builder in an obscure part of the Roman Empire. Lord, you endured thirty years of this petty existence, surrounded by people whose lives hinged on nothing more than menial work and a peasant's concern for where the next meal was coming from. You know exactly what it is to endure life's banalities.

Whatever we are given to endure, be it darkness or merely twilight, the Lord will, at the end of time, return in a brilliance which will illuminate all things. Then, if we have abandoned our spark of divine fire and become one with the gloom, this light of Christ will be an unbearable intrusion. But if there is still a glow within us, we will leap for joy at his coming to rekindle our flame, and we will become truly one with the eternal divine light.

If we only allow the Holy Spirit, the divine wind, to fan our spark of fire we will keep it aflame in readiness for Christ's Second Coming. Otherwise our spark will surely die.

I am reminded of the words of the Russian St Seraphim of Sarov. 'God is fire… When we feel a chill in our hearts from the devil – for the devil is cold – let us call on God. He will come and warm us with perfect love… and at the touch of this fire Satan's chill will vanish.'

Our true calling as Christians is to be 'little Christs', unquenchable lights shining vividly in the darkness and the twilight. Lord, let me be all flame!

29-51. *Expectation*

The Second Coming is spelt out in this passage in terms of expectation. 'Be prepared!' Christ tells us. We don't know when he is to return but we should await the day eagerly and with sober anticipation.

The extent to which that anticipation has been lost can be seen by recent pronouncements on the Second Coming in the press. It just isn't going to happen, we are told by the cynics. They will have none of churchy scaremongering. The Master is not only delayed, he has abandoned his trip altogether. And I use the word 'trip' deliberately because it is in such belittling language that the cynics rail against those they label simple-minded in their faithful acceptance of the Gospel.

Of course, if you believe Jesus is really rotting in some undiscovered tomb and only lives on in the spiritual afterglow of his followers, then there is clearly no one to return. But for those of us who know that is not the case, to truncate his message is to destroy it. 'My words will never pass away', Christ tells us himself. There seems to me little point in struggling to keep the precepts of the Sermon on the Mount if one considers the rest of his message worthless. Why not eat and drink with the drunken like the rest of society? Why cling to a never-never land when present reality is so concrete?

Can we really trust the Gospel? the sceptics say. Can we really trust in Christ, can we really trust that there is a God at all?

What does God say to that?

'Can I really trust human beings, or are they going to let me down as soon as I'm out of sight?', he says to us here.

But the beauty of it is that God does trust us. He has trusted us to remain faithful until he comes again, faithful in deeds and faithful to the truth of his word that he will indeed come with great power and glory.

The cynics are reciting nothing more than the old line 'it will never happen to me'. 'Oh yes it will, just when you least expect it', Christ reminds us, shaking his head.

Lord, grant us expectation, with sobriety of heart but also with great joy at the promise of meeting you!

Chapter 25

Awaiting the Kingdom

1-13. Watching with the bridesmaids

Complacency is such a subtle tool of Satan. It comes very often dressed up in the most sophisticated garments but in reality it is as foolish as these stupid bridesmaids. Yet it takes us in again and again.

We know how the Early Church stood watchful, expecting the return of the Lord at any moment; and we recognise that after two thousand years our ears are no longer pricked for the Bridegroom's coming this very night.

No. We assume the world will muddle on as a matter of course, and even discount the possibility of our own sudden death, despite accident statistics.

There is another side to our complacency. We don't see the need to be watchful because we feel certain of Christ's welcome for us whenever he happens to come. No matter if we are nodding off over our spluttering lamps; this parable can't mean us, we churchgoers are as good as inside the bridechamber already. It is the unbelieving mob around us which needs to watch out.

Isn't that just the sort of counsel the serpent gave Eve? Take no notice of God's warning words, he doesn't really mean it. All through the Bible, all through history, Satan whispers to humanity 'You will not die', and like fools we prefer to believe him rather than Christ, who warns us, 'yes, you will unless I give you new life.'

It seems to me pointless to read this parable confidently identifying with the wise bridesmaids. The Lord is directing these words at all of us who await his coming, we are each called to prepare ourselves and stand alert. It is no use being given a place in the Kingdom if we are asleep when the Kingdom comes.

14-30. *Responding in gratitude*

I am struck by something fresh in this passage: how our lives – and our eternal lives – depend on our personal relationship with God.

What he entrusts to each of us is utterly individual and what we are called to make of it is also individual. I am not just thinking of what we mean by the modern word talents but of the essence of our relationship with God.

We all respond to him according to the development of our own potential. If I relate to him as a reluctant slave to a taskmaster, concerned only with his power to tyrannize, I will be impervious to his mercy at the Judgement. The mean-hearted person will remain closed to God's generosity of spirit, both in this world and the next.

There is a lovely saying: 'In eternity everything capable of growth will grow.' Even if we only had a very small seed of divine love within us in this life, so long as we have enabled it to sprout a little it will continue its ever-upward journey towards the light of Christ in the Kingdom. But if the seed has not been planted in fertile soil but has withered and been buried, have we not already in fact entered that outer darkness?

The thought which vividly came to me when I read of God's concern for the sparrow fallen to earth was that none of us is worthless in his eyes. Yet here Christ himself talks ominously of the worthless slave – one who had denied his own worth. What are we to make of that?

Surely that for just such worthless slaves as we are, Christ has paid his life – which is not theological speculation but fact. We are certainly all worth less than that price, and yet it has already been given for us.

We cannot understand, only marvel in gratitude and

respond. Gratitude was something radically absent from the third servant. He saw God only in the legalistic terms of what he considered fair trading; he was completely closed to the concept of the undeserved free gift.

But that is precisely what we have all received. Apparently worthless, each of us has been given the price tag of Christ's own worth. Our response can only be gratitude.

31-46. The Kingdom of love

The parable of the sheep and goats is built on the divine principle of love – the love each one of us is called to show to the image of Christ in our neighbour. Without love, how can we be integrated into his Body, in whom there is no evil, no absence of good, no unlovingness? So we must start now to rid ourselves of everything which still separates us from this love.

This parable blows away every idea of faith versus works. We are saved by one thing only: love, God's love for us and our love in response. If we have truly entered into the mystery of this love-relationship we are already of the Body of Christ, one with him for eternity. If our lives have been built on anything less, then we are outside this mystery of love, the Kingdom, both now and forever, because we have set up a 'great gulf' between God and ourselves by our failure to participate in his love. If we have not actively loved him in our neighbour we will not want to love him face to face because there will be absolutely nothing on which we can build a relationship with him. So our decisive encounter with him will be hell.

Lord, help me to see you in every person I meet today, even in those who are apparently unlovely. Help me to remember that whatever I do for another is done for you. Lord, help me to grow in love, so that my human love can truly participate in the divine. Lord, help me to live your eternal life of love now!

Part 7

THE PASSION

Chapter 26

Passover

1-16. Gratuitous love

The clouds darken as this fateful week progresses. The religious leaders assemble in the palace of Caiaphas the high priest to plot Jesus' death.

Against this tense background we are given an interlude which seems at first not to be related. A woman anoints Jesus as he dines at Bethany.

The other Gospels furnish us with slightly more details: she is a 'sinner', a woman of ill repute, whose action might have had erotic connotations: 'she hasn't stopped kissing my feet since she came in', Christ says to his affronted host. It all seemed rather distasteful, if not shocking.

But the Lord sees beyond appearances. He recognises her heartfelt repentance, her joy at being forgiven and the love this awakens in her heart. 'She loved much', Christ says, and the phrase is not without its irony. Oh yes, she had certainly 'loved'; that had been her profession. But now she has discovered the real meaning of love, of which Simon still has no idea.

It is not only their host who is put out by her actions. The disciples also object; for a different reason. They see her gesture of love as just a gesture – empty, pointless and stupidly wasteful. The money could have been put to much more practical, 'pious' use.

St John tells us that it was Judas in particular who complained and that his motive was not concern for the needy but sheer avarice. He had become a slave to money. Outwardly he had control of the common purse, but the truth of it was that the purse had come to control him. Like so many of us. Why does everything in my life have a price?

Why does mindless generosity such as this woman's still strike us as a self-indulgent aberration? And yet – is it not these apparently empty gestures which are so central to Christianity? In less than a week another anointing will be undertaken. This time the women who come to Christ's tomb, not to perform a symbolic ritual but the real thing, the last rites for a corpse, will be the channels for the Resurrection message. How would we have heard the Good News if they had not set out on their mission of useless but loving generosity? This completely gratuitous love, free from any ulterior motive, free from all our customary calculations – nothing but an overflowing of burning self-giving – is it not akin to God's love for us? Is this not where the divine and human meet, in a communion of the kind of love that transcends all our usual limitations?

17-35. *The Last Supper*

The Last Supper is one of the most puzzling and mysterious events in history. In a sense it is so familiar: depicted a thousand times in religious paintings so that the image of the long table with Jesus sitting centre stage, the Twelve flanking him, is etched into our minds. It is, of course, a totally false image. The Gospel actually says they reclined, in the manner of the ancients; this was no Renaissance banquet, nor were the participants all ranged conveniently on one side facing an unseen audience.

So we know, but we do not know, how to imagine the scene. In the same way we know, but we do not know exactly what was done and said, and when, and why. Matthew's account appears straightforward; but we have to reconcile it with John's. All the little but important details have to be pieced together, and it is not easy. Even then we can only guess at the atmosphere of joy, of sorrow, of surprise, of foreboding which filled the Upper Room.

What comes over to me is the intensity: the depth of the disciples' horror at the prospect of betraying their beloved Master; the stunning moment when Christ turns the Passover upside down and proclaims the New Covenant; the dread experience of this undreamt-of communion which compels a guarded public description of perhaps the most private moment in their lives. For the sake of future generations they have to spell out the last intimate meeting with Christ, the last occasion when they can speak with him, share his presence, be at one with him in a new and unforeseen way. In a matter of a few hours the memory of this hallowed event will be stained by their desertion of him, as their words of devotion are given the lie in the darkness of Gethsemane. All this emotional irony the hapless evangelist has to set down, without losing the divine message in the sorry historical record. There is a terrible pain here, among the joy of celebration.

Each of us can identify with Peter and his denial at some time in our lives. At spiritually charged moments we make rash promises with a courage which is born of all our Godward longings. Blinded by faith in our own strength we do not see Christ shaking his head in sorrow. None of us can predict how we will react when our backs are to the wall. Our assertions come not from divine foresight but from our own wishful thinking.

If we do not even understand ourselves, our limitations and our false presumptions, how can we possibly understand the ways of God? We cannot reconstruct with absolute accuracy the details of the Last Supper, nor discern from the Gospel passages the precise significance of everything that was said and done. Christians disagree among themselves what Jesus meant by his Body and Blood: memorial, symbol, the real thing? There is no way that this dread evening can be pieced together with the sort of historical reliability we crave. All we can say with certainty is that all his life Jesus was surrounded by misunderstanding, and that we should be wary of imagining that we

173

are totally free of it because we live in the time after Pentecost. The Spirit blows where it wills, and that is not always in our direction.

How, then can we discern any meaning for us in the Last Supper? Perhaps we have to lay aside the very notions of discerning and understanding.

Christ did not tell us to seek explanations but to eat and drink. 'Participate', he says to us. It is not by reconstructing this evening in the fashion of scholars that we will gain insight, but by accepting his invitation to enter the Upper Room week by week and be present at his Table.

What I know of Communion is not through understanding but by experience. It is not an abstract idea to be discussed and studied, not a theological argument, but a reality of which I am certain because I have taken part in it. I have experienced something of the closeness, of the pain, of the joy, of the mystery, according to my own extremely limited capabilities. I can read this passage, come to the Eucharist and participate in my inner depths in truths of which one cannot speak in words.

This is what the Lord offers to each of us. He invites us personally to the Wedding Feast of the Kingdom, he stands at the door of the Upper Room and beckons us in. He is the Door; he is the servant who washes us in preparation; he is the celebrant of the Paschal sacrifice; and he is the Lamb, slain for us, the sacrifice poured out for our salvation. All this we know not from reading about a distant event in history but by accepting his invitation to participate.

And we also know that he is the One who leads us out of this mysterious chamber, back into the darkness of the world, to stand with us and suffer on our behalf as time and again we forget our pious promises and take to our heels as soon as danger threatens. All we can do is weep at cock-crow, and turn back towards his loving gaze, remembering that the Door to the Upper Room is always open, awaiting our return.

One can hardly dare write any words about the awesomeness of Gethsemane. None of us can put ourselves in Christ's shoes and approach the depths of his horror at what lies before him, nor understand his dread and victorious struggle to join the will of humanity with the will of God.

We would like to think, however that we are at least capable of standing by in solidarity with him in his isolation; yet we know from this passage that even his closest disciples could not do that. In the cool night air Christ, alone, waits and watches for the torchlight procession which will herald his betrayal.

I can imagine the scene because I have been there. One can still see the gnarled olive trees whose predecessors sheltered the Lord. I stood in their shade, meditating on Christ's betrayal, in pious fashion as a pilgrim should.

Suddenly one of our party, less 'pious' and more excitable than I, rushed past me looking for her husband. And as she ran she shouted out, 'Christ, where is he?'

That blasphemy in such a hallowed place cut me to the heart. Was Christ betrayed again, today? It brought tears to my eyes.

Then I thought: how many times had I, in other places, betrayed or abandoned him? Was there ever an age in which he has not been betrayed?

The cutting edge is, of course, the fact that Christ was betrayed by a friend. Indeed, he reminds Judas that he is not just on amicable terms but has been chosen by him as a friend. Even at this moment of betrayal, he calls Judas into friendship.

We, too are chosen by Christ to be his friends. Our response depends on our free will but the initiative comes from him. And what do we make of this divine friendship?

Another thought: the kiss, sign of Judas' treachery, might well have become for the Church a universal sign of betrayal. Yet it was incorporated into the Church's ritual as the kiss of peace, and this is still used today. What a mystery! What a wonder, that this gesture could by the blood of Christ be cleansed and given new life, new meaning!

57-75. *The world gone mad*

The whole of the Passion narrative is shot through with the most terrifying irony. Here we see Caiaphas – high priest according to God's own Law, by a heredity appointed by him in much the same way as we saw Christ's heredity sketched out at the beginning of the Gospel – come face to face with the very God he claims to serve, and declare him to be false. He who adjures Christ 'by the living God' has the Living God condemned to death.

An irony on another level: in 1993 archaeologists in Jerusalem unearthed the family tomb of Caiaphas and identified the skeleton of an elderly man as probably the high priest himself. If only his minions could have done the same with Jesus, recovered his corpse as a public refutation of the resurrection rumour!

I cannot imagine what it must be like to gaze at the bony fingers which rent the priestly garments in mock horror at 'blasphemy', or the empty sockets from which the eyes glittered in moonlit triumph as Christ was condemned. All one can say is that skull was never as sightless as at the moment when it looked upon Light eternal and experienced nothing but the darkness of hatred.

Irony runs through my Church's service texts appointed to accompany the reading of this passage: 'He who loosed Adam from the curse is bound; the Creator is struck by the hand of his creatures; he who tries the hearts of men is unjustly tried.' Everything is stood on its head. The madness of evil reigns. The evening which started out so awesomely beautiful in the Upper Room has become the ultimate nightmare.

Into that scenario a bewildered Peter is projected. We

176

can talk about his unaccustomed cowardice, his shameful denial, his total failure towards his Master only within the honest realisation that, on the night of God's supreme solidarity with humanity, no one dared show solidarity with him.

How many times have I in a mocking spirit called on Christ to prophesy? How many times have I tried to blind-fold him while I got him back for not acting according to my dictates? How many times have I in embarrassment or fear pretended not to know him? We can all, like Peter at the Supper, make rash promises born of romantic ideals, only to see our true everyday selves unable to carry them through.

And have I wept? Have I not hoped instead to find a quiet resting-place out of his gaze, like Caiaphas? And will not all things hidden be, like the high priest's skeleton, eventually revealed?

Lord, the world is mad, and I am caught up in this madness. I too have shared in that night of darkness, of momentary triumph of evil over good. Lord, bring me to my senses, that I may weep bitterly over my deeds.

Chapter 27

The crucifixion

1-10. *Judas*

I find the figure of Judas almost impossible to imagine. We are told little about him, apart from the fact that he was in charge of the finances and was dishonest in this task. It's as if everything else about him – not just his virtues but his very personality – had been swallowed up and he had become a money-bag on two legs. Nothing else mattered to him.

Until it was too late. In a moment of horror he suddenly saw the total emptiness of serving Mammon and betraying God, and it destroyed him.

How far does this apply to us? We who live in the luxury of the Western world, who see nothing wrong in betraying the world's starving for the price of a second car or a foreign holiday, have surely not really listened to the parable of the sheep and goats.

Today I can forget that my love of money and possessions destroys the needy, but do I realise that it is Christ himself who is my victim? And when at last I do see that I am killing not the indestructible God but myself, will it be too late?

'Too late' were the words that confronted Judas, as they are said to confront all those who find themselves at the gates of hell. Lord, bring us to our senses now, before it is too late!

11-31. *God seized and bound*

It is highly unfashionable nowadays to believe in Satan. Devil-worshippers apart, recognition of the existence of and personification of evil is decried as an unhealthy and stupid leftover from the Middle Ages.

Evil itself is hardly acknowledged in our society. It is not politically correct or socially acceptable. People and events are victims of circumstance, not of some malevolent force.

The weak and the foolish and the cynical do not need head-on temptations like Jesus in the wilderness; they are pushovers in their blindness, led by the nose by Satan who uses their unwillingness to acknowledge him as a means of enslavement.

It has happened before, decisively. Judas' example we have just read. Here we see the chief priests and elders, long-time enemies of Christ, turning the hearts of the people who once loved him. The irony continues: 'Barabbas' means 'son of the father', and this rogue is reprieved while the true Son of the Father is condemned to death. Pilate, knowingly doing wrong, thinks he can absolve himself with an empty gesture. The masses, ignorant of the mercy of God, think they can call down full responsibility on to themselves and unborn generations. Everyone is unaware that it is in God's hands alone to condemn or forgive, and that by submitting in silence to their dreadful decisions he is offering his own blood as an absolution for all.

The final irony: the King of Kings, robed in the garments of derision, lacerated, blood-spattered, bruised, half-dead from the most vicious torture – all that is conveyed in the little word 'scourged' – is rendered a totally pathetic and degraded figure, and in this condition offered mock homage.

Does not the same thing happen today, when Jesus is reduced by the scoffers to a wimpish figure fit only for the cruellest lampooning? Do we not witness this scene regularly in the media, and do we not, like the disciples, tiptoe quietly away?

I can only ever read these words in horror that humanity could have turned on God and sought absolute triumph over him. Yet I may only rightly feel that horror if I am prepared to include myself, as I truly am, within humanity.

32-45. *Murdering God*

We have arrived with Jesus at Golgotha. Certain details of the crucifixion which we learn from the other Evangelists are absent here: the plea of the good thief, 'Remember me, Lord when you come in Your Kingdom'; and Jesus' words as he is nailed to the cross, 'Father, forgive them, for they know not what they do.'

Who were his crucifiers? There has been much finger-pointing throughout Christian history, mostly in one direction. The Roman soldiers just doing their job could be let off the hook but the Jews, standing there in mockery, having consciously taken Christ's blood-guilt on their race in perpetuity, were another matter.

That wicked nonsense has been the shameful rationale for the most hideous crimes in the past. The Apostles, the embryo Church gathered at the first Pentecost, all the brave men and women without whom Christianity would never have got off the ground – all these would have fallen under the same blanket condemnation.

So were Christ's crucifiers only those who literally plotted his death that fateful Passover? That too is wrong.

Continuing my thoughts from the preceding passage, the truth – too horrifying for most of us to stop and consider – is that the blanket covers the whole of humanity. Both collectively and individually we are all responsible, by our sinfulness, for the crucifixion. Every time we turn aside from God, preferring our own will to his, every time we attempt to obliterate Christ from our presence while we commit some misdemeanour, we are placing ourselves on the side of the crucifiers.

Was this not indeed Adam's sin, the original sin shared by all humanity: the urge to 'murder' God, to deny him and to usurp his place? In the Old Testament that is only a shadow, but at the Incarnation it becomes a real possibility. The awareness of the writers of Genesis of the human compulsion to blot God out reaches its dread conclusion.

Humanity seeks primarily to control. We have found our place on earth as the dominators of the natural world, intellectually unchallenged, the manipulators of knowledge and the laws of the universe. Humanity has learnt to play God, and has become hooked on the game.

In this scenario the real God is a terrible stumbling-block, for whose blood we bay. We have tried to control him with our religious formulae. But the Holy Spirit blowing where he wills is an offence. Alas for us! One cannot thrust a spear into a spirit. But God in the flesh can be bound, nailed and speared, to our satisfaction. Adam's sin is fulfiled literally, historically but we all share in the fulfilment just as we all share in Adam's prefiguring.

But that is not the end of the story. This blanket condemnation which we so lightly call down upon ourselves is taken on by Christ himself, as in an action too amazing for us to comprehend he drapes it over his own shoulders and, in the ultimate act of love, dies clothed in our sins and our hatred. He dies our death to save us from our self-induced Godlessness at the very moment of our total rejection of him.

What if Jesus had come down from the cross as the scoffers demanded? The world would have been condemned to live under the perpetual tyranny of a God who, when it came to the crunch, had insufficient love to die for his creatures. Certainly we would be spared the anguish of doubting him, for his continuous presence would crush unbelievers under a loveless despotism of the type Satan offered Christ. Instead of Satan's triumph over God we see in the crucifixion his defeat, and the victory of the Trinity of Love.

Lord, in our blackest moments we scoff, we make demands, we revile you constantly. We delight to see you hanging in torment, suffering the punishment which should be ours. We share in the darkness of the scribes and Pharisees, the chief priests, the easily-led crowds, the unfeeling, unthinking Romans, the unrepentant thief. We share in the cowardice of the apostles, the faithlessness of all who had pledged allegiance to you while the going was good. We have no words or acts by which to redeem ourselves. But you have redeemed us by sharing and taking on our sins, even to death. O Lord, glory to you!

46-54. *Death*

The crucifixion is an event of cosmic proportions. The sun hid its light, the rocks split asunder; the whole creation was literally shaken at the dread mystery of seeing its Creator on the cross. Christ died not only for humanity but for the salvation and restoration of the whole cosmos.

The Word, at whose voice all things came into being, cries out in dereliction and the earth returns to its primeval darkness. In an unfathomable way, Christ himself shares our life and death to its bitterest end by partaking of the terrifying experience which is the tragic human lot: the darkness of separation from God.

In our attempt to put God to death we put ourselves to death as we cut ourselves off from his presence. Jesus, the perfect Man, the Messiah, God Incarnate, himself takes on our utter desolation and shouts the cry of every one of us at some time in our lives: 'My God, my God, why hast Thou forsaken me?'

How can God lose the awareness of his own divinity? How can the Son lose his eternal oneness with the Father? We can only gasp in great awe at his acceptance of this ultimate catastrophe and its inevitable consequence: death.

The self-emptying which Christ took on at his nativity reaches its fulfilment as he shares this death of ours with all the frightening limitations of being human. He alone of all humanity remains faithful to God, yet he takes on our faithlessness and dies, as we all do, of the loss of God. And in doing so, in descending into hell, the place of godlessness, he destroys it. As the Orthodox Easter hymn puts it, Christ 'tramples down death by his death'. His Passover sacrifice of himself becomes the new Passover from death to life, and he takes us fellow humans by the wrists and drags us through the narrow gate with him.

But that is to look ahead to the resurrection, as even the most pious of us cannot help doing. What of his followers on the first Good Friday? Did they endure the darkness with him? They were enveloped in the world's darkness, in that isolating individuality which is so often ours; not sharing the Lord's darkness but intent only on their own situation. When it comes to us today, do we endure it as his darkness?

Living with resurrection hindsight, can we learn to transfigure even our most Godless moments with the light of Christ's solidarity?

55-66. Burial

In moments of crisis the weak often become strong, and vice versa. Here we see courage and faithfulness displayed not by the inner circle of the Twelve but by an outsider and by the women.

All through the Gospel women have played a vital role. St John tells us that he stood at the foot of the cross with Christ's Mother. She who uniquely knew who he was, who had at the beginning of his Incarnation offered him to his Father in the Temple in a sacrifice which she knew would one day be literally fulfilled, stands pierced herself by the sword of human hatred which pierces him.

'Perfect love casts out fear', St John tells us in his first epistle. This little group rises above the instinct for self-preservation in order to carry out the last act of love for their Master, small consolation for his death but in the circumstances the only way left to them to give their all. And that is all the Lord asks; it will be enough to herald the Resurrection.

Part 8

CHRIST IS RISEN!

Chapter 28

The Kingdom come with power

1-15. The Resurrection

Whichever Gospel one reads, there is something strange about the Resurrection narratives. It is not just the odd discrepancy. More than that, they are an anticlimax to the drama and detail of the accounts of the Passion.

It is almost as if we were there in the darkness with the two Marys, picking our way over unfamiliar ground, catching a glimpse of this or that in the Passover moon before being enveloped again by the gloom of unknowing.

And that is odd. One might have expected the central event of Christianity to be set out in suitably resounding language like the Nativity. One might have expected a definitive version, couched in poetic terms and ringing with descriptive certainty as the faith of the Early Church rang with certainty.

One might have expected, in other words, a doctored account – not the garbled words of confused eye-witnesses but a pat, 'official' text couched in the experience of the Holy Spirit and the hindsight and understanding of established Christianity.

The result would have been tidy and impressive, not the breathless incoherence of a handful of dazed individuals. It would have been satisfying on a literary level, dignified and moving. It would have been a glorious statement – but not a message; not the Good News blurted out in amazement and near terror, which is what the women brought back from the empty tomb.

There are no Gospel attempts to describe what was not

humanly witnessed, the Resurrection itself; it was a sacred, mysterious moment shared only in the communion of the divine Persons of the Trinity. The evangelists have rightly respected that mystery and have not tried by poetry, symbolism or well-meaning invention to re-create what it was not given to humanity to know.

What they do describe – and describe so tantalisingly scrappily, we are tempted to think – is the aftermath: Jesus alive, risen in body and soul as the complete Man, the conqueror of death and its glorious first-fruits.

To those people who claim the Resurrection story to be a 'myth' couched in the picture language of a resuscitated corpse symbolic of a continuing spiritual message, dare I say, read it again? This is no concocted story made to dress up some vague religious fervour. It is awkward, unpolished, one could even say unsatisfactory. But it obstinately refuses to go away.

What we have here is not a grand finale to the Gospel message but a beginning: the beginning of new life, of a new relationship with the Lord Jesus Christ which looks outwards from the empty tomb into the glory of the divine light.

16-20. A new beginning

The final verses of St Matthew's Gospel set the seal on all that has gone before. The risen Lord Jesus Christ, standing with his disciples gathered around him, declares his eternal authority. He sends them out to baptize all nations and promises his perpetual presence to us all.

How beautiful! But do we know the truth of this from our own experience? When I think of moments of prayer, of receiving Communion, of God-given circumstances, of seeing his presence radiating from other people, I know it to be so.

Yet I have only to turn back one thin page of my Bible and I am again face to face with the cross, and with Jesus' own cry of forsakenness, reminding us starkly that in this 'always' in which he promises to share is included all the moments of pain and horror of the human condition, even moments like his when we will feel totally cut off from the awareness of that presence.

And yet... To be baptized is to die with Christ, to be merged into his death and to be reborn into the eternal life of the Kingdom. This promise which Jesus makes to his disciples has already become reality in *us*. We *are* baptized, we have already, incipiently, passed beyond death and have entered this Kingdom's new life. It has been planted within us as a seed; and, nurtured by the continual presence of the Holy Spirit, it will grow and grow.

So the end of the Gospel, like the Resurrection, truly becomes a beginning. Just as the Church's year is a never-ending cycle of feasts, so our Christian life is one of continual re-living, re-learning, re-reading the Gospel in an ever-deepening consciousness given by God. Having come to the end it is with great thirst for more, for a closer acquaintance with the Lord and his words of life, that I am eager to turn back to the first page and begin again.

I am baptized, but I have not yet learnt to observe all that Christ has commanded. Like the disciples, I need to return to Galilee, to the beginning of the relationship, to where they and I first came to know him.

Even then, according to verse 17, there are still people who see all, and yet doubt. How could we see the crucified yet risen Lord bodily before our eyes and still not believe? The capacity of the human heart to remain closed to God, and his respect for that, is awesome.

'Blessed are the pure in heart, for they shall see God.' It is only by observing all that Christ commanded, by learning to live by the purity of the Gospel message, that our eyes will truly see.

O Lord come with us, be with us always and guide us in all your commandments, that we may truly stand before you to behold the beauty of your face. Amen.

Epilogue

The word 'Gospel' means 'Good News', and news is something with which we are bombarded daily in a variety of ways. We buy newspapers, we turn on the television or radio. We receive personal news via letters and phone calls or word of mouth.

All this is a process of taking, of receiving something from an outside source, generally referred to as 'hearing'. 'Have your heard about so-and-so?' we often say, as we pass on the latest piece of tabloid extravaganza. But we take it and pass it on in an indifferent way. It remains external to us. Whether it elates or depresses it is usually on a level which we could broadly call entertainment. We take it in with our ears but we don't take it to heart.

That has not been my experience of reading the Good News of the Gospel. Have I taken hold of the words, or have they taken hold of me? Have I not given – given something of myself – as well as received?

There is one sort of news we receive which often involves giving: a party invitation. Whether it's a 'bring a bottle' rave-up or a formal wedding, we don't go up empty-handed. We give, and we give joyfully, wholeheartedly, gratefully.

The Gospel is an invitation: not just to read about the life of Jesus of Nazareth, nor to learn a set of moral rules and religious truths, but to participate in our Father's house in the banquet of eternity. We are not asked to bring our share of the refreshments, nor an expensive present. The only gift we can offer to God is the one he has given us – our lives, our whole selves, body and soul, clothed in the shining garment of the Holy Spirit.

We hear this invitation repeated in words in the Gospel.

We could perhaps think of our baptismal certificate as the invitation card itself. It does not have R.S.V.P. on the bottom, but is not 'repondez' – respond – its most vital message?

Respond! Come! Become! – citizens of eternity, new creatures, grains of salt and rays of light pouring out on to the world to give it the abundant life that only Christ can offer. Whatever we have received from the Gospel, let us be so transfigured by it that we cannot help giving it to our neighbour, that together we may enter the Kingdom.